# Assertiveness, Boundaries and Conflict Management

ABC Workbook

F. Russell Crites, Jr.

© Copyright Revised 2019 All rights reserved. All rights reserved. No part of this publication may be reproduced, stored in a retrieval system, or transmitted in any form or by any means: electronic, mechanical, photocopy, recording, or otherwise, without prior written permission of the copyright owner.

Published by CPC Dallas, Texas.

Printed in the United States of America

Library of Congress Cataloging-in-publication Data.
Crites, Jr. Floyd. Russell

ISBN: 9781533465832

Assertiveness, Boundaries and Conflict Management: ABC Workbook / F. Russell Crites, Jr.

Self Help for Adults

Second Edition

The strategies, techniques contained in this book are not intended as a substitute for consulting with you mental health provider. In addition, this work is being sold with the understanding that neither the author nor the publisher is engaged in rendering medical, nutritional (including supplements), or psychological advice or diagnosis. Neither the author, nor the publisher shall be liable for any loss, injury, or damage allegedly arising from any information or suggestions in this book.

Orders can also be obtained by calling 972-506-7111 or by going to Amazon.com. Orders of five or more workbooks at a time from the author get a 40% discount and can be resold for client use.

For grammatical consistency and clarity, the pronouns "he", "his" and "him" have been used throughout instead of "she or he", "his or her" and "her and him." No sexual bias or insensitivity is intended.

## Acknowledgements

I would like to give thanks to a number of people who reviewed this workbook, gave feedback and in general made it more usable. Special thanks to Robert, Anjana, and Michiko for their suggestions and assistance. I would also like to thank dozens of clients who have made use of this information, who in tun gave me feedback about how to make it more user friendly. I appreciate each and every one of you.

# Table of Contents

## Section One: Foundation for Change     11

- ➤ What You Think is What You Become     13
- ➤ The Inner Sanctum     14
- ➤ Going to the Movies     18

## Section Two: Assertiveness     19

- ➤ Assertiveness Defined     21
- ➤ Three Types of Behavior     22
- ➤ Major Blocks to Assertiveness     23
- ➤ Assertive Techniques     24
    - Broken Record     25
    - Broken Record II     27
    - Fogging     29
    - Negative Assertion     31
    - Active Selective Listening     33
    - Passive Selective Listening     35
    - Standing Firm     37
    - The Assertive Delay     39
    - The Negative Inquiry     41
    - Content to Process Shift     43
    - Free Information     45
    - Self-Disclosure     47
- ➤ Assertive Techniques Situation Worksheet     49
- ➤ DESC Scripts     50
- ➤ Developing a DESC Script     52
- ➤ Assertive Scripts     54
- ➤ Assertive Script Writing Worksheet     55
- ➤ Assertive Script Writing and Guided Imagery     56
- ➤ The Three Step Technique     58
- ➤ The Three Step Technique Worksheet     59
- ➤ Do's and Don'ts for Assertive Behavior     60

## Section Three:  Boundaries                              61

- Boundaries                                                                63
- You May Need to Set Boundaries if                                         65
- Two Great Boundary Killers                                                66
- Boundary Weaknesses and Your Personal Code                                68
- Preliminary Guidelines to Boundary Setting                                76
- Guidelines for Boundary Setting                                           77
- Boundary Truisms                                                          78
- Boundaries and Responsibility                                             79
- Prepare for Boundary Violations                                           80
- Minimize Unhealthy Relationships                                          82
- Five Boundary Areas                                                       84
- Self-Image Model and Boundaries                                           85
- Self-Image Review and Handout                                             86
  - How Mental Boundaries are Damaged                                       88
  - Setting Healthy Mental Boundaries                                       89
  - How Social Boundaries are Damaged                                       90
  - Setting Healthy Social Boundaries                                       91
  - How Physical Boundaries are Damaged                                     92
  - Setting Healthy Physical Boundaries                                     93
  - How Spiritual Boundaries are Damaged                                    94
  - Setting Healthy Spiritual Boundaries                                    96
- Feelings and Boundaries                                                   97
- Boundaries and Self                                                       98
- Boundaries and Personal Relationships                                     99
- Boundaries and My Family                                                  100
- Boundaries and Friends                                                    101
- Boundaries and Work Situations                                            102
- Personal Boundaries                                                       103
- My Boundaries Worksheet                                                   104
- Boundary Weaknesses and Your Personal Code                                105
- Other-Oriented Overt Control and Boundary Damage                          106
- Other-Oriented Overt Control and Boundary Damage Worksheet                108
- Other-Oriented Covert Control and Boundary Damage                         109
- Other-Oriented Covert Control and Boundary Damage Worksheet               111

- Self-Oriented Overt Control and Boundary Damage — 112
- Self-Oriented Overt Control and Boundary Damage Worksheet — 114
- Self-Oriented Covert Control and Boundary Damage — 115
- Self-Oriented Overt Control and Boundary Damage Worksheet — 118
- Reducing Self-Oriented Control Issues — 119
- Common Yet Effective Boundary Statements — 121
- Boundary Consequences and Considerations — 122
- When Boundaries Don't Work — 123

# Section Four: Conflict Management — 125

- Preventing Conflict — 127
- Steps for Addressing Conflict — 128
- Rules for Conflict — 129
- Reduce Conflict Triggers — 130
- Self-Monitoring by Frequency for One Behavior Per Week — 132
- Learn to Listen — 134
- Active Listening Skills — 135
- Non-Verbal Listening Skills — 136
- Keep Yourself Under Control — 137
- Strategies for Inner Peace — 138
  - Your Vacation Paradise — 139
  - The Chair: Breathing and Relaxing for Healing — 141
  - The Quick Relaxation Technique — 142
- Feelings and Conflict Resolution — 143
- Non-Productive Conflict Styles — 144
- Addressing Non-Productive Conflict Styles — 145
- Time Outs for Conflict — 147
- Resolution, Compromise or Management — 151
  - Conflict Resolution Methods — 152
  - The Learning Conversation — 153
  - The Communication Game — 154
  - The Five Step Conflict Resolution Technique Described — 157
  - The Five Step Conflict Resolution Technique Worksheet — 158
  - Conflict Resolution and Decision-Making Worksheet — 160
  - Problem Solving and the Two Column Technique — 161

- Problem Solving and the Two Column Technique Worksheet — 162
- Compromise Methods — 163
- The Will to Compromise — 164
- Compromise Model for Conflict Management — 166
- Compromise Model for Conflict Management Worksheet — 168
- Conflict Management Methods — 170
- Conflict Management Method Options — 171
- Keeping Track of Decisions — 172
- Conflicts with Personal Decision Making — 174
  - Seven Step Problem Solving Method — 175
  - T-Chart for Decision Making — 176

## Appendices — 177

- Coping Styles Assessment Quick Check
- Coping Styles Assessment Quick Check Summary
- Developing a DESC Script
- Assertive Techniques Situation Worksheet
- Assertive Script Writing Worksheet
- The Three Step Technique Worksheet
- My Boundaries Worksheet
- Other-Oriented Overt Control and Boundary Damage Worksheet
- Other-Oriented Covert Control and Boundary Damage Worksheet
- Self-Oriented Overt Control and Boundary Damage Worksheet
- Self-Oriented Covert Control and Boundary Damage Worksheet
- Fixing Boundary Issues Worksheet
- Addressing Non-Productive Conflict Styles Worksheet
- Self-Monitoring by Frequency for One Behavior Per Week Form
- The Learning Conversation Worksheet
- Five Step Technique Conflict Resolution Technique Worksheet
- Conflict Resolution and Decision-Making Worksheet
- Problem Solving: The Two Column Technique Worksheet
- The Will to Compromise Worksheet
- Compromise Model for Conflict Worksheet
- Decision Making T-Chart Worksheet

**Recommended Readings** — 209
**Other Works by this Author** — 211

# Author's Note

Whether it be lack of knowledge about how to deal with issues in your life, codependency issues, or other behaviors that are causing you to have life difficulties, you can learn how to address them using the tools you find in this work. Failure to be assertive when needed, failure to set healthy boundaries or a lack of being able to resolve conflict in some way can cause you serious difficulties in all aspects of your life. The purpose of this work is to provide you the tools you need to better take care of yourself in the face of conflict, even if it's minor. It will address, 1) how you can be more assertive, 2) how you can set healthy, appropriate boundaries for self, personal relationships, your family, friends, work situations and more, and 3) multiple conflict resolution, compromise and management strategies.

Any unhealthy behavior can be addressed using the materials in this workbook. This includes codependent behaviors that many people are experiencing. Even if you don't think you have any possible codependent issues you may want to take the 'Coping Styles Assessment Quick Check' in the appendices of this work. The Coping Styles Assessment Measures nine family of Origin Roles, twelve codependencies, four unhealthy communication styles, twelve unhealthy family rules past and present, and determines if any of three underlying motivations are present. Using all this data, a four-letter code is identified. Once identified, you can purchase a 90 page (approximate) code workbook that addresses most of the issues identified in the assessment. Once you know your code you will be able to purchase the codebook that is most appropriate for you. Each codebook is a workbook covers all the issues measured by the assessment and is about 90 pages long.

**Boundary Issues and the Coping Styles Assessment**

The last three letters of you code will also help you identify specific boundary problems you may be having. Certain worksheets and Information found in this workbook requires that you know your CODE. If you don't you will not be able to take advantage of some of the information presented. It is suggested that you take the assessment. It will provide you with information that can help you see why you think and act the way you do. Regardless, other information found in this work can be of extreme benefit if diligently work through it.

## Book Suggestions for Assertiveness

Three books have a tremendous amount of information regarding assertive skills, DESC scripts and resolving conflict. The first is a book titled, <u>When I Say No, I Feel Guilty: How to Cope, Using the Skills of Systematic Assertive Therapy</u> by Smith, M. J. This was one of the first books written on assertiveness and continues to be a wonderful resource for all who are interested. Mr. Smith identified 12 specific assertive skills. They are addressed in a very practical ways in the ABC workbook.

The second book that has much needed information about assertiveness and specifically DESC scripts. It was written by Bower, A., Bower, G. and is titled, <u>Asserting Yourself: A Practical Guide for Positive Change.</u> This book is also a great resource if you need additional information about how to write scripts, how to use them in a variety of situations and a lot more. Some information from this book has been adapted for use in this ABC workbook.

The third book is titled, <u>Difficult Conversations: How to Discuss What Matters Most</u> by Stone, D., Patton, B., & Heen, S. This is one of he most powerful books I have read that shows you how to address conflict as it occurs. It should be a must read for everyone. One conflict resolution method was adapted from this book for use in the ABC workbook.

All three of the above mentioned works would be great additions to anyone's library.

# FOUNDATION FOR CHANGE

## Section One

Change is necessary if you are going to be able to stand up for yourself and others. As you begin this workbook, one of the most important things that you must accomplish is not with what you learn from or write within these pages, it is whether you are willing to utilize your inner self for change and development. So, before we begin looking at specific issues you have as a result of poor assertive skills, poor boundaries or difficulty in handling conflict, it is vital that you develop an understanding of how you can truly change from within. To do this we will be offering you the option of using the Inner Sanctum and Going to the Movies to increase your success.

- What You Think is What You Become        13
- The Inner Sanctum        14
- Going to the Movies        18

# What You Think is What You Become

Internal change is necessary if you want to become a person who naturally is assertive, sets good boundaries and is capable of handling conflict well. You must teach your mind that you want to be, not just know the desired skills. You want these new skills to be a natural part of you. To do this you have to flood your mind with the skills you want to have within you. What you think about, what you listen to, what you see or visualize, what you have embedded in your brain via any medium pre-determines what you say and do each minute, hour and day of your life. You can change what you 'naturally' think, or how you handle things on a day-by-day basis by simply changing what you feed your mind daily. In 1903 James Allen wrote a powerful little book entitled, As a Man Thinketh. In this book he stated, "*A man is literally what he thinks, his character being the complete sum of all his thoughts. As the plant springs from, and could not be without the seed, so every act of a man springs from the hidden seeds of thought, and could not have appeared without them. This applies equally to those acts called "spontaneous" and "unpremeditated" as to those which are deliberately executed.*"

In 1960 Maxwell Maltz, M.D., F.I.C.S. wrote a book entitled, Psycho-Cybernetics: A New Technique for Using your Subconscious Power. Basically, he believed that your mind has a servo-mechanism inside of it that is goal-striving in nature. It is both impersonal and automatic. Simply stated, the goal of this servo-mechanism is to give you what you are asking for. Your mind determines what you want and how you will respond as it receives images, thoughts, and words that you feed it. As soon as these messages are processed by the mind it seeks to make happen what has been internalized. Basically, if you flood your mind with what you want, e.g. an assertive skill, a healthy boundary, effective conflict management, the skills or knowledge will become part of you. You must feed your mind this information over and over until it becomes part of you, not just some techniques you are learning. That's why using guided imagery or the Going to the Movies strategy is so helpful. If you flood your mind with the skills you want to have, in time they become a part of you. So that is your task. You don't just want to learn strategies or techniques. You want to internalize a new way of handling issues so that your natural response will be healthy. The Inner Sanctum is a tool that will help you accomplish this.

# Visualizing Your Inner Sanctum

What is the purpose of the Inner Sanctum? One foundational truth is that for true change to occur you must change from the inside out, not just change behaviorally. The Inner Sanctum is a fun method by which you can change from within using a variety of methods.

Visualizing your Inner Sanctum is the first step in this process. It is from this place that you will create your home base for everything else that you do when you visualize. All other visualizations will follow your entrance into this place. This is certainly optional, but it is a very powerful tool once you create your personal Inner Sanctum.

Here are some things that many people have decided to have in their Inner Sanctum. You can pick what you want or be creative and add anything else that would help you in any way.

- A stage with a large screen behind it
- Door to Your Relaxing or Peaceful Place
- A very relaxing chair
- Door that Returns you to Your Present Location
- A nice size couch and chair
- An extra door to be used for special activities
- And whatever else you want….it can be one room or multiple rooms.

NOTE: Keep in mind that some people have a lot of difficulty being able to 'see' images in their mind, especially when they are in color or have detail. If this is a problem the person can attempt to think what is happening instead. If it is too frustrating, most of these Inner Sanctum strategies can be completed without using the Inner Sanctum.

---

Close your eyes and begin to totally relax your body. You are about to embark on a journey that will change your life for the better. Imagine yourself sitting where you are right now. As you visualize yourself, you see a door of energy appear in front of you. In your mind, you get up to explore where this door leads to. When you walk through the energy door, you find yourself in a beautiful meadow. To the north you see a path. You begin to walk down the path experiencing a peace of mind that you haven't felt in a while. The very surroundings seem to make you relax and feel peaceful. As you continue to walk, you see a large archway and a door beyond it. You go to the door and it opens easily as you push it. The room is old and obviously hasn't been used for years. You see some stairs that lead downward across the room through a door. As you walk down the stairs, you begin to experience a deep feeling of relaxation--of peace. This place could very well be a place for you to get away to where you can be alone and at peace. With each step, you become more and more relaxed--you feel better and better about what you will find. You come to a large ornate door that is locked. As you look around, you notice a strange key partially lying under a book on the table next to the door. When you use the key, it unlocks the large ornate door. You walk through the doorway and see a beautiful room. It has in it all the things that you need to relax and feel good about yourself. It was as if someone had especially made this room for you. You close the door and lock it knowing that no one can get in your room unless you allow them. You are perfectly safe, at peace and relaxed in your room. As you look at the wall to the right, you notice that there are more energy doors. Above one there is an inscription that states, 'This is a doorway to a place of serenity, calm and peace.' The sign above the next doorway states, 'This is a doorway to your past; use it wisely.' Next you see a doorway with an inscription that simply states, 'Reality!' This door can be used for quick trips to and from your Inner Sanctum if you do not desire to walk your way in. Only you can use this door unless you allow others to use it. When you want to enter it from the outside all you must do is say a secret word to yourself and you will instantly step through this doorway in your Inner Sanctum where you can do whatever needs to be done at that time. You need to determine what that secret word will be. You can change the word any time you like. Last, you see a doorway that has no sign over it. It may be used in the future, but not right now. On the wall, straight in front of you as you enter by the ornate door you see a short stage with a huge blank screen much like you would see in a movie theater.

There is a large comfortable chair just to the left after you enter the room. It has all kinds of gadgets on it that will help you in the future. Sit in the chair and simply look around the room. You will see a couch and a chair directly in front of you that faces the movie screen. Take in all that is currently in the room and determine if there is anything else you want to add. You can have anything in your Inner Sanctum that you want. You can also change things up any time you want to. Once you are finished relaxing for a few moments, listen to your breathing and be at peace. When you are ready to come back to reality you may do so by going through the 'Reality' door or you can unlock your large door walk up the steps, down the path and into the door in the meadow. In either case when you walk through the door of energy you will find yourself where you were before you entered your Inner Sanctum.

**Options:** Think about it for a moment. Is there anything you would like to put in your Inner Sanctum? Remember, this is a place of healing, peace and sometimes learning. However, you can put things in your Inner Sanctum that would make it more comfortable for you. What might those things be?

### Inner Sanctum Basic Design

```
┌─────┬──────────────────────────┬─────┐
│     │  Stage with Movie Screen │     │
│     └──────────────────────────┘     │▓ Door to
│                                      │  Vacation
│                                      │  Paradise
│                                      │
│                                      │▓ Door to
│                                      │  Your
│                                      │  Past
│                                      │
│                  ▭  ◗                │▓ Door to
│                                      │  Reality
│                                      │
│        ◖                             │▓ Door to
│     Relaxing                         │  Optional
│      Chair                           │
└──────────────▓───────────────────────┘
               Door to
            Inner Sanctum
```

What would you like to add? How would you like to configure it? As long as you have the necessary items it doesn't matter what your Inner Sanctum looks like. Draw your own picture of what your Inner Sanctum would look like if you want.

## Methods for Change or Relaxation in the Inner Sanctum

Here are some ways you can use the Inner Sanctum to help you learn, develop skills, change your inner self, or simply to relax.

1. Using the large video screen, you can watch video clips of specific skills that you want to develop. This should include auditory feedback. You can see body language, hear words, tone, etc.
2. You can use the stage to play out scenarios. When you do this, you can see yourself stepping on the stage and working through a scenario. Watch yourself handle a situation well that up to now has been a problem. Watch yourself utilize a specific assertive skill and see yourself use it exactly as it should be handled. Watch yourself set a boundary and be comfortable setting it. All the above includes your words, tone, emotions presented, body language, etc.
3. You can use the Chair to relax so that you won't overreact due to uncontrolled stress.
4. You can use the last door to the left on the right wall as you step in your door, to go to your personal Vacation Paradise where you can be at peace, be happy and totally enjoy your time away from it all. It could be:
   - You on the Beach at your favorite place (Make it up if necessary).
   - You sitting on the porch of a mountain cabin overlooking a beautiful meadow.
   - You sitting with your back against a large bolder as you look over a still, glass like lake with a majestic mountain behind it.
   - You anywhere you want to be that helps you relax.
5. You can also use your Assertive Script Writing and Guided Imagery strategy and incorporate it into the Inner Sanctum.
6. You can also use the Assertive Technique Situation Worksheet to mentally practice a specific assertive skill.

Any of the assertive techniques, strategies for boundaries or conflict skills can be played out on the screen or on the stage. Your options are few and the possibilities are vast.

# Going to the Movies

Going to the Movies is a technique that can be used in the Inner Sanctum or it can be used while relaxing. Going to the Movies calls for you to develop a Video Clip in your mind that shows you using a specific skill that you want to improve. It may be an assertive skill, a specific boundary that you need to be able to communicate, a way of handling a specific conflict or any other issue you may have that requires a specific response that you would prefer. Going to the movies is most effective when you include a visual image, movement, auditory input, feel touch, experience feelings, etc. In other words, you want to make the video clip as real as possible. It's as if you are practicing it in real life. Put yourself in the picture. Make it as real as you can. Become a participant in the video clip….don't just watch it.

Step One: Identify the purpose for using Going to the Movies, e.g., a behavior that you want to change, a skill you want to develop.

Step Two: Go to the Inner Sanctum and you can watch the scene play out on your screen or you can go into a relaxed state and simply play it out in your mind.

Step Three: Once relaxed see it, hear it, experience the video clip of you successfully using the assertive skill, setting the boundary, or working through a conflict for about 5 to 10 seconds.

Step Four: Now start it over. You can rerun it over and over depending on what you need. Remember to use as many senses as possible.

> *Did You Know*
> *Your mind cannot tell the difference between*
> *Imagination and Reality.*

Why is the statement above important to you? It's because when you use visual imagery, **especially when you get as many senses involved as possible**, it can be very powerful for learning, developing skills, relaxation and change. *Going to the Movies* is a strategy that helps you do just that!

# ASSERTIVENESS

## Section Two

It is often more difficult to maintain progress than it is to actually deal with life issues. This workbook will help you learn the skills that you need so that you can maintain your progress and not fall back when pressures arise. "I know what I should be doing, but for some reason I seem to fail when it comes to standing up for myself or in doing what is right." How many times have you said this to yourself when you thought you had your problems overcome only to find out that in reality they have beaten you again? Wouldn't it be great if you knew what you needed to do to make sure that you were successful…that you could stand up for what was right because you had the tools that allowed you to do so? Well, there are three basic tools that you need to internalize if you are to be successful. If you haven't developed these skills, then you are doomed to failure when you face life's difficulties.

1. You must learn how to stand up for your rights, how to be assertive.
2. You must learn the skill of setting up and maintaining boundaries. Boundaries should not be rigid, or weak and easily destroyed or walked over.
3. You must learn the art of conflict management. This includes learning to resolve, compromise and manage conflict as it occurs in your life.

When you have developed these three skills you will be prepared to face the conflict that comes to you on a daily basis. This first section will discuss some helpful assertive skills that you need to be able to stand up for yourself. The areas to be discussed in this section are:

- ➢ Assertiveness Defined — 21
- ➢ Three Types of Behavior — 22
- ➢ Major Blocks to Assertiveness — 23
- ➢ Assertive Techniques — 24
  - Broken Record — 25
  - Broken Record II — 27
  - Fogging — 29
  - Negative Assertion — 31
  - Active Selective Listening — 33
  - Passive Selective Listening — 35
  - Standing Firm — 37
  - The Assertive Delay — 39
  - The Negative Inquiry — 41
  - Content to Process Shift — 43
  - Free Information — 45
  - Self-Disclosure — 47
- ➢ Assertive Techniques Situation Worksheet — 49
- ➢ DESC Scripts — 50
- ➢ Developing a DESC Script — 52
- ➢ Assertive Scripts — 54
- ➢ Assertive Script Writing Worksheet — 55
- ➢ Assertive Script Writing and Guided Imagery — 56
- ➢ The Three Step Technique — 58
- ➢ The Three Step Technique Worksheet — 59
- ➢ Do's and Don'ts for Assertive Behavior — 60

# Assertiveness Defined

## Assertiveness: A Definition

Being **assertive** means that you are able to use assertive techniques that will help you take a stand regarding, 1) your own rights, and 2) other people's rights. You do this in a calm and positive way, without being either aggressive, or passive.

## Six Key Points Regarding Assertiveness

1. Being assertive means that you stand up for your own rights.
2. Being assertive means that you stand up for the rights of others.
3. Being assertive means that you don't act passive or use passive statements.
4. Being Assertive means that you don't act aggressive or use aggressive statements.
5. Being assertive does not mean that you cannot be kind, soft, nice or empathetic when you communicate. This is especially true when you initially set up new boundaries with someone.
6. Being assertive does mean that you stand up for boundaries you have established. This is often the time that you are a bit more forceful and communicate consequences for boundary testing or violations. Follow-through regarding consequences is essential or there is no sense in establishing boundaries.

# Three Types of Behavior

There are three basic types of behavior. Each type has its own characteristics. Only one of them is truly healthy.

**PASSIVE:** The passive style of behavior calls for the person to stay in a submissive position. Passive people rarely stand up for themselves and usually end up suffering silently when someone has taken advantage of them. Such people often blame others for their miserable lot. However, the real problem is that they refuse to stand up for their personal rights and lack the strength and/or tools to take responsibility for their own lives and stand up for themselves.

NOTE: If you have an "O" in your Personal Code, then you are probably passive, shame-based or other oriented. You must take the Coping Styles Assessment to get the code. It is in the appendices.

**AGGRESSIVE:** Aggressive behavior usually, if not always, injures to win. As a result, individuals who use aggressive behavior are usually out to hurt the other person physically or emotionally to make sure that he gets what he wants. So, you can see aggressive behavior is used to exalt one person at the expense of the other. In relationships where there is an aggressive person, he must be in total control most of the time.

NOTE: If you have an "S" in your Personal Code, then you are probably aggressive, control based or self-oriented. You must take the Coping Styles Assessment to get the code. It is in the appendices.

**ASSERTIVE:** Assertive behavior focuses on negotiating reasonable changes via rational, realistic communication to equalize the balance of power in the situation. The purpose of assertive behavior is to assure that you get what is rightly yours in all situations or to protect you from those who would take advantage of you in any way.

*Keep in mind that Boundaries work hand in hand with good assertive skills and help protect you.*

# Major Blocks to Assertiveness

Here are some blocks to assertiveness. Put a check next to any of the below blocks to assertiveness that you feel you may be experiencing.

\_\_\_\_\_**Lack of knowledge:**  A lack of knowledge regarding specific assertive skills or methods and how to use them obviously produces problems for being assertive.

\_\_\_\_\_**Negative Self-Image:**  A negative self-image can contribute to a lack of confidence as you deal with people in different situations. A poor self-image produces a very superficial or uncertain person who has little chance of handling life's demands well.

\_\_\_\_\_**Fear of Conflict Situations:**   There are two basic reasons why people experience fear of conflict.  1) Because they know that they will inevitably lose the battle; they don't attempt to deal with the problem. 2) Because they have never been taught that it's okay to stand up for themselves and don't have the tools to do so.

\_\_\_\_\_**Poor Communication Skills:**   Poor communication skills is also a block to being assertive.  If you feel uncomfortable with your ability to communicate effectively it will be difficult for you to stand up for yourself in a crisis situation.

\_\_\_\_\_**Poor Boundary Setting:**   Boundary setting is the limits you set for yourself that can be defended using assertion and conflict resolution skills. If you don't even know what your boundaries are, it becomes extremely difficult to become assertive or to seek conflict resolution.  Boundaries are essential in the process of assertion.

\_\_\_\_\_**Poor Conflict Resolution Skills:**   If you don't know how to handle conflict when it occurs assertive skills by themselves often are not enough. That is why it is important that you know how to handle conflict using several conflict management techniques.

# Assertive Techniques

There are multitude of assertive techniques that can be used to handle life's problems. Smith, in his book entitled, *When I Say No, I Feel Guilty: How to Cope, Using the Skills of Systematic Assertive Therapy,* identified twelve specific assertive skills that can help you in a variety of different situations. The list below are the assertive techniques addressed in this workbook.

- Broken Record
- Broken Record II
- Fogging
- Negative Assertion
- Active Selective Listening
- Passive Selective Listening
- Standing Firm
- The Assertive Delay
- The Negative Inquiry
- Content to Process Shift
- Free Information
- Self-Disclosure

Try to determine which assertive techniques would be most beneficial. Work through them all and decide if there are two or three that really seem to work for you. You can always refer back to the others as you have need, but learn how to really use your top three well. Practice them for small things and the larger ones will get easier to address in time.

NOTE: There is a worksheet immediately after the last assertive technique. It's called, **Specific Assertive Techniques Situation Worksheet**. There is also a copy in the appendices so that you can have a copy to use over and over if needed.

# Broken Record

The broken record is a skill that calls for you to calmly repeat what you want over and over again without letting the other person change the subject on you. This method teaches persistence that many of us do not have when under pressure. As you practice this skill, you will find that it will become easier to stick to your end goal without giving in to pressure, arguments, criticism or any other sidetracking tactic.

**Situational Usage:** This is used when you rightfully need something from a person or when someone has promised something.

Example:

John "You said we could work on the garage today. Can we start soon?
Mary "I don't feel like it today."
John "You said you would help today; I really need your help!"
Mary "Can't we do it tomorrow."
John " We have already put it off two times. You said you would help today, and I really need your help now."
Mary "Oh, all right, I guess we can do it now!"

**Your Scenario**

Identify two or three situations where someone has said they would help you in some way but seemed to back out of it when the time came to help.

**Scenario #1:**

**Scenario #2:**

**Setting Up Broken Record for Your Situation**

Pick two situations that often occur and identify a Broken Record statement that you can use. You can work through your third and others using Specific Assertive Techniques Situation Worksheet as desired.

Situation:

Broken Record Statement:

Situation:

Broken Record Statement:

# Broken Record II

The second way you can use the broken record is to identify a consequence that in some way relates to the problem you are experiencing. First, you tell the person what you need, want, etc. Second, you tell them again making sure that they hear you the second time. In addition, you also communicate a consequence if the person does not respond in a favorable way. Basically, you are being assertive and setting a boundary all at the same time. As you practice this skill, you will find that it will become easier to stand up for your rights without having to given in to others.

**Situational Usage:** This is used when you are experiencing a problem with a person right now….in the moment and you want it to stop.

Example: John has been continually asking Mary for a date--she's interested, but he seems to be pressing her for more time and she's not ready for that intense a relationship. Actually, she's tired of his calling all the time.

John  "How about letting me take you out for dinner tonight?
Mary  "Thank you, but not tonight!  Maybe some other time."
John  "You said we could go out again soon.  Let's make it tonight!"
Mary  "I am interested in going out with you again at a later date. However, when people press me, I find that I have no desire to spend time with them. If you would like, call me in a couple of weeks."

## Your Scenarios

Identify two or three situations where someone has said they would help you in some way or made a promise, but seemed to back out of it when the time came to help or follow-up.

**Scenario #1:**

**Scenario #2:**




**Setting Up Broken Record II for Your Situation**

Pick two situations that often occur and identify a Broken Record II statement that you can use. You can work through your third and others using Specific Assertive Techniques Situation Worksheet as desired.

Situation:



Broken Record II Statement:



Situation:



Broken Record II Statement:

# Fogging

Fogging is a skill that helps you learn how to accept manipulative criticism by calmly acknowledging that there may be some truth to what your critic is saying. This allows you to maintain your own belief system about self and others yet takes the joy of putting others down away from those who are negative.

**Situational Usage:** This is used when a person is saying things about you that *is not true,* but you don't want to get into an argument or discussion with him.

Example:

John "You really are a procrastinator! It really bugs me that you can't do what you say you are going to do."

Mary "You know….that may be true. I guess I ought to think about that. Thanks, I appreciate you sharing that with me."

NOTE: The word **MAY** means that it could be true, but in this case it is not. You just don't confront his error. **Ought** to think about it also suggests that you agree, but in fact you don't.

**Your Scenarios**

Identify two or three situations where someone has been unjustly critical, abusive, mean, etc. Think about a time when you were in an uncomfortable situation.

**Scenario #1:**

**Scenario #2:**

**Setting Up Fogging for Your Situation**

Pick two situations that often occur and identify a Fogging statement that you can use. You can work through your third and others using Specific Assertive Techniques Situation Worksheet as desired.

Situation:

Fogging Statement:

Situation:

Fogging Statement:

# Negative Assertion

Negative Assertion is a skill where you learn to accept your mistakes and faults by strongly agreeing with hostile or constructive criticism of your unwanted or negative qualities. This does not mean that you should be apologizing for anything. It simply means that you agree with others when they are being critical and let them know that you certainly believe that they have a point. This deflates anger and criticism that comes from others.

**Situational Usage:** This is used when a person is saying things about you that *may very well be true,* but you don't want to get into an argument or discussion with him.

Example:

John "I'm sick and tired of your being lazy around the house. You're getting lazy and fat and I can't stand it."
Mary "You know, there is some truth to that! I may need to work on those problems. Thanks for letting me know what I need to work on."

**Your Scenarios**

Identify two or three situations where someone has said they would help you in some way but seemed to back out of it when the time came to help.

**Scenario #1:**

**Scenario #2:**

**Setting Up Negative Assertion for Your Situation**

Pick two situations that often occur and identify a Negative Assertion statement that you can use. You can work through your third and others using Specific Assertive Techniques Situation Worksheet as desired.

Situation:

Negative Assertion Statement:

Situation:

Negative Assertion Statement:

# Active Selective Listening

Active selective listening calls for you to tell a person that you will not respond to them if they talk to you in an abusive or critical way. It sets boundaries up front and lets the person know what types of communication you will accept and what you won't accept.

**Situational Usage:** This is used when a person is saying things to you that are critical, abusive, mean, or negative in any way. You tell them you won't respond to such communication.

Example:

John "If you weren't such a stupid moron, we would be able to work out this problem."
Mary "I will not respond to you if you use unkind, critical or abusive words. It's your choice."
John "I don't care what you say. You're going to listen."
Mary DOESN'T RESPOND, IGNORES HIM!!!
John "You can't get away with not talking with me forever--you're just being pigheaded."
Mary DOESN'T RESPOND, IGNORES HIM!!!
John "Oh, all right, may we please sit down and discuss this in a calm way."
Mary "I'd be glad to as long as you don't talk to me critically or abusively."

**Your Scenarios**

Identify a situation where someone has said they would help you in some way but seemed to back out of it when the time came to help.

**Scenario #1:**

**Scenario #2:**



**Setting Up Active Selective Listening for Your Situation**

Pick two situations that often occur and identify an Active Listening statement that you can use. You can work through your third and others using Specific Assertive Techniques Situation Worksheet as desired.

Situation:



Active Selective Listening Statement:



Situation:



Active Selective Listening Statement:

# Passive Selective Listening

Passive selective listening calls for you to simply ignore someone when they talk to you in a negative, abusive or critical way. You don't let them know why, you don't tell them anything. You simply don't respond until they communicate in a healthy, non-abusive way. This can be used often after you have set a healthy boundary using Active Selective Listening.

**Situational Usage:** This is used when someone is speaking to in a disrespectful, angry, abusive, or critical way. You simply ignore the person until he says something positive and constructive or you can walk away. You don't tell them why.

Example:

John "If you weren't such a stupid moron, we would be able to work out this problem."
Mary DOESN'T RESPOND, IGNORES HIM!!!
John "You can't get away with not talking with me forever--you're just being pigheaded."
Mary DOESN'T RESPOND, IGNORES HIM!!!
John "Oh, all right, may we please sit down and discuss this in a calm way."
Mary "I'd be glad to."

**Your Scenarios**

Identify a situation where someone has said they would help you in some way but seemed to back out of it when the time came to help.

**Scenario #1:**

**Scenario #2:**

**Setting Up Passive Selective Listening for Your Situation**

Pick two situations that often occur and identify a Passive Listening statement that you can use. You can work through your third and others using Specific Assertive Techniques Situation Worksheet as desired.

Situation:

Passive Selective Listening Statement:

Situation:

Passive Selective Listening Statement:

# Standing Firm

This technique calls for you to develop an awareness of how the controller tends to bait you into defending yourself. Recognize that no one can continue a verbal attack if only one person is involved in the conversation. If you respond by defending yourself or by counterattacking, you have just fallen into their game. They have won. In addition, if you participate in this dysfunctional communication, you are letting this person get away with controlling you again. Once you begin to realize how controllers get you to respond to inaccurate and often faulty information, you can begin to overcome their abuse. There are three basic steps to this technique. First, you simply ignore the bait. Second, you only respond to the hidden meaning behind the attack. Third, your response must always be, "I will not play verbal games with you--so don't even try to control me in that way. Then walk away!

**Situational Usage:** This is used when people try to control or bait you to respond to their verbal attacks. Ignore the bait, communicate that you don't communicate with people who speak to you that way and walk off.

Example:

John "If it weren't for you, we wouldn't be having these problems."
Mary "I can't accept that. If you can identify real problems that need to be addressed, I will be glad to discuss them." Walk away if he continues.

**Your Scenarios**

Identify a situation where someone has said they would help you in some way but seemed to back out of it when the time came to help.

**Scenario #1:**

**Scenario #2:**

**Setting Up Standing Firm for Your Situation**

Pick two situations that often occur and identify a Standing Firm statement that you can use. You can work through your third and others using Specific Assertive Techniques Situation Worksheet as desired.

Situation:

Standing Firm Statement:

Situation:

Standing Firm Statement:

# The Assertive Delay

This technique calls for you to learn how to avoid having to respond to someone immediately when you are being pressured. It may be a simple time out that lasts for fifteen minutes, or it may be for a day. However, you choose to set a time that is convenient for you until you are ready to give a response, and not before. Take time to determine what the person wants, gather information if needed or do whatever you feel is necessary to ready yourself for a response. There are three basic steps to this technique. First, you simply acknowledge the persons statement or question. Second, let them know that you need time to respond. Third, tell them when you will talk to them about it and disregard their attempts to get you to respond immediately. Walk away if necessary or if possible!

**Situational Usage:** This is used when you don't want to respond to a person when you are pressured to give an answer or respond.

Example:

John "You know there are times that I really believe you intentionally make others mad."
Mary "I need time to think about that. I'll get back with you and we'll discuss it."
John "I want to discuss it now!"
Mary "I can't discuss it until I think about how I might be making others mad. I'll let you know when I'm ready to discuss it." Walk away and do something else if necessary.

**Your Scenarios**

Identify a situation where someone has said they would help you in some way but seemed to back out of it when the time came to help.

**Scenario #1:**

**Scenario #2:**

**Setting Up the Assertive Delay for Your Situation**

Pick two situations that often occur and identify The Assertive Delay statement that you can use. You can work through your third and others using Specific Assertive Techniques Situation Worksheet as desired.

Situation:

The Assertive Delay Statement:

Situation:

The Assertive Delay Statement:

# The Negative Inquiry

This technique calls for you to actively seek criticism of your behavior. However, you only do this when you have a good response ready. An effective response can overcome many critics. If it doesn't, you can use some of the other techniques that you have learned. There is another benefit of Negative Inquiry that can be very helpful to you. Sometimes you will learn that the 'critic' was just blowing off steam and that he didn't really mean what he said, so he will admit it when you use the Negative Inquiry.

**Situational Usage:** This is used to actively seek out the reason for criticism or negativity. If the person apologizes, you go on. If they don't, you can use other Assertive Techniques to address the issue.

Example:

John "You really can be bossy at times and I don't like it?"
Mary "How do you see me as being bossy?"
John "Oh, you're really not bossy, I'm just upset with my boss at work. He's been a pain this week."

(If you believe that there is some truth to what this other person is saying, you can determine if it is really a problem that you need to work on. If it isn't then you can tell him that he has a right to his opinion, but it's obviously wrong and you don't want to hear it from him again. If he uses it again, then you can use Active or Passive Selective Listening.)

**Your Scenarios**

Identify a situation where someone has said they would help you in some way but seemed to back out of it when the time came to help.

**Scenario #1:**

**Scenario #2:**

**Setting Up the Negative Inquiry for Your Situation**

Pick two situations that often occur and identify The Negative Inquiry statement that you can use. You can work through your third and others using Specific Assertive Techniques Situation Worksheet as desired.

Situation:

The Negative Inquiry Statement:

Situation:

The Negative Inquiry Statement:

# Content to Process Shift

When you use the Content to Process Shift, you are changing from the topic to an analysis of what is going on between the two of you. You have identified that the person is not upset about what he is talking about, but instead he is upset about old issues. When you perceive that this is going on you may want to do a Content to Process Shift to deal with the real issues.

**Situational Usage:** This is used when a person seems to be reverting to a historical issue that is upsetting him. Ask him to address the current underlying issue rather than history.

Example:

John "You really can be bossy at times and I don't like it?"
Mary "It seems to me that we are getting away from the issue we were discussing. You've switched on me and are now discussing old issues! Right now, you appear to be angry at me. What's causing this?"


**Your Scenarios**

Identify a situation where someone has said they would help you in some way but seemed to back out of it when the time came to help.

**Scenario #1:**

**Scenario #2:**




**Setting Up Content to Process Shift for Your Situation**

Pick two situations that often occur and identify a Content to Process Shift statement that you can use. You can work through your third and others using Specific Assertive Techniques Situation Worksheet as desired.

Situation:




Content to Process Shift Statement:




Situation:




Content to Process Shift Statement:

# Free Information

Free information is a skill that helps you develop a recognition of cues given by others in every day conversation. This information directs you toward what is interesting or important to that person. As a result, you develop a greater ability to be effective in social communication. It's only assertive in the sense that you encourage a free exchange of information.

**Situational Usage:** This is used to help you share some of yourself and get to know another person. It helps you identify what is important to that person which leads to better communication.

Example: Getting to know another person!

John "I really love Chinese food. (Free Information.) What kind do you like the most?" (Prompting for Free Information)
Mary "I like Chinese food, too, but I think I like Italian even more."(Free Information)


### Your Scenarios

Identify a situation where someone has said they would help you in some way but seemed to back out of it when the time came to help.

**Scenario #1:**

**Scenario #2:**




**Setting Up Free Information for Your Situation**

Pick two situations that often occur and identify a Free Information statement that you can use. You can work through your third and others using Specific Assertive Techniques Situation Worksheet as desired.

Situation:



Free Information Statement:



Situation:



Free Information Statement:

# Self-Disclosure

Self-Disclosure is a skill that allows you to freely communicate both the positive and negative aspects of yourself. This accomplishes two things. First, it frees you from the negative feelings that you may have had about your 'weaknesses'. Second, it shows the other person that you can admit that you have weaknesses, and it makes it easier for him to communicate at a deeper level.

**Situational Usage:** This is used to share weaknesses about yourself that in turn often causes the other person to feel more comfortable sharing with you at a deeper level.

Example: Two people who are beginning to get to know each other.

John  "There are times that I really feel that I need to work on being more punctual. It's really a problem for me sometimes."
Mary  "You weren't late to pick me up today!"
John  "I know! I'm proud of myself! I just want you to know that my goal is to be punctual with you!"
Mary  "That's really nice! I know that it's hard to change the way you are. I'm impressed that you are willing to work on things like that."

## Your Scenarios

Identify a situation where someone has said they would help you in some way but seemed to back out of it when the time came to help.

**Scenario #1:**

**Scenario #2:**

**Setting Up Self-Disclosure for Your Situation**

Pick two situations that often occur and identify a Self-Disclosure statement that you can use. You can work through your third and others using Specific Assertive Techniques Situation Worksheet as desired.

Situation:

Self-Disclosure Statement:

Situation:

Self-Disclosure Statement:

# Assertive Techniques

## Situation Worksheet

Instructions

1. When you are faced with a situation you need to address using an assertive technique you can use this worksheet.
2. Identify the situation.
3. Pick the Assertive Technique that you want to use.
4. Write a statement that addresses the issue using the chosen assertive technique.

| **Assertive Techniques Situation Worksheet** |
|---|
| **Situation Described:** |
| **Specific Assertive Technique to Be Used:** |
| **Assertive Statement:** |

A copy of this form is in the Appendices.

# DESC Scripts

There are four basic steps in developing a D(escibe) E(xpress) S(pecify) C(onsequence) script. Whenever you are faced with a situation where you feel you might be controlled or manipulated by another person, use script writing to help you.

Example: To visit a lawyer who has just started working on a case for you.

**Describe:** I have been attempting to contact you by telephone for four days now concerning my case. I was told that you would get back to me as soon as possible.

**Express:** It is very important that I give you further input if you are going to represent me in this matter. I also feel that it is important that we have ongoing communication, but for some reason you have chosen to not communicate with me.

**Specify:** It is essential that you call me immediately!

**Consequence:** If I don't talk to you by tomorrow at 12:00, I will assume that you are not interested in my case and I will go elsewhere for assistance.


**Summary Statement for the DESC**

In this case the DESC was written into a letter. You may do this or simply use it as a verbal response to any unacceptable situation. It is usually better to have written and practiced your DESC script before you verbally communicate it. Here is a DESC script.

Dear Mr. Jones,

I have been attempting to contact you by telephone for four days now concerning my case. I was told that you would get back to me as soon as possible. It is very important that I give you further input if you are going to represent me in this matter. I also feel that it is important that we have ongoing communication, but for some reason you have not chosen to communicate with me. It is essential that you call me immediately! If I don't talk to you by tomorrow at 12:00, I will assume that you are not interested in my case and I will go elsewhere for assistance.

                Sincerely Yours,

                Joe Sample
                Phone #: 1-800-354-9910

## Scenarios for a DESC Script

Identify three scenarios where you could use a DESC script and briefly describe each scenario below.

## Scenarios Briefly Described

1.

2.

3.

# Developing a DESC Script

There are four basic steps in developing a D(escibe) E(xpress) S(pecify) C(onsequence) script. Whenever you are faced with a situation where you feel you might be controlled or manipulated by another person, use script writing to help you.

Instructions:

1. Write one of your scenarios below from the previous page.
2. Complete he DESC below to show how you would address this issue.

**Your Scenario:**

**Describe:**

**Express:**

**Specify:**

**Consequence** (Choose positive or negative or both):

**Write Your Personal DESC Script**

Instructions

Write your personal DESC script based on the Scenario show on the previous page.

**DESC Script**

A copy of this form is in the appendices.

You can practice your script using the **Assertive Script Writing and Guided Imagery** or **Going to the Movies** strategies to make it more natural for you to use. These two strategies are in this workbook.

# Assertive Scripts

Assertive Scripts are slightly different from DESC scripts and can be used for controllers, compliants and avoidant individuals to help them overcome their codependent nature. Below is an example of how an assertive script is set up. This case shows how a compliant can set up a healthy script.

Step #1. Name the Situation!
Step #2. Name the Person you want to alter a situation with.
Step #3. Describe the setting--the place it usually takes place
Step #4. Write down what you usually say to them.
Step #5. Write down a counter script that states exactly what you want to communicate. You can include the persons normal response that is unacceptable if desired.

Example of an Assertive Script

Step #1: I never get to decide where we eat when we go out.
Step #2: My husband.
Step #3: Usually at home in the early evening or just before lunch on the weekends.
Step #4: Wife: "Honey, I know you usually want to pick where we eat. However, I really want to go to that Italian restaurant tonight."
Step #5: Husband: "Sorry. I would really like to go someplace else."
Wife: "Well, I really have my heart set on Italian food tonight. I would love for you to go with me, but I guess I can just go alone and you can go where you want. If you change your mind let me know. I'm leaving in about ten minutes."

Pick two situations you would like to develop an Assertive Script for.

1.

2.

# Assertive Script Writing Worksheet

Instructions

1. Describe the situation in the space provided below.
2. Name the person you want to alter the situation with.
3. Describe the setting--the place it usually takes place.
4. Write down what you usually say to them.
5. Write down a counter script that states exactly what you want to Communicate. You can include the persons normal response that is unacceptable if desired.

| | **Assertive Script Writing Worksheet** |
|---|---|
| Step #1. | Describe the Situation! |
| Step #2. | Name the Person you want to alter the situation with. |
| Step #3. | Describe the setting--the place it usually takes place. |
| Step #4. | Write down what you usually say to them. |
| Step #5. | Write down a counter script that states exactly what you want to Communicate. You can include the persons normal response that is unacceptable if desired. |

A copy of this form is in the appendices.

# Assertive Script Writing and Guided Imagery

Imaged script writing is a very powerful tool for change. This technique helps you establish new patterns for dealing with events that are unhealthy or uncomfortable. There are eight steps that make up a good script. Let's look at each step so you can see what you must do to write a good assertive script.

Step #1: Determine the situation that you need to change or avoid.
Step #2: Write a specific scenario that alters the event in a positive way.
Step #3: Go to your Inner Sanctum and relax in your chair.
Step #4: See the new scenario played out successfully on your screen or stage. Play out the scene five times or until it becomes natural. Remember to use as many senses as you can. It's more powerful.
Step #5: Relax and enjoy the feelings that come from successfully dealing with this issue.
Step #6: Return to reality feeling surer of yourself--knowing that you have a plan and that you can overcome this problem.
Step #7: Take the first opportunity to use your new script. Check how strong your tendency is to go back to the old script.
Step #8: Repeat going to your Inner Sanctum and practicing your new successful scenario as needed.

Example: An individual is having difficulty with sobriety. For years he has stopped at a local bar on the way home. Although he wants to quit, and has repeatedly said that he won't stop and get a drink on the way from home, his good intentions usually don't make it past the bar. This can be accomplished with or without the Inner Sanctum.

Step #1: I have trouble drinking and can't seem to stop drinking at the local bar after work.
Step #2: After looking at a map I determine a new way to go home that doesn't have a bar on the way. I will drive straight home without stopping.
Step #3: Go to your Inner Sanctum and relax in your chair. Take some deep breaths and let yourself relax for a few minutes.

Step #4:   Visualize yourself taking the new route home. I see myself going straight home, not stopping anywhere. When I get home I walk up to my wife and tell her that I love her. (See the new scenario played out successfully on your screen. Play out the scene five times or until it becomes natural.)

Step #5:   Relax and enjoy the feelings that come from successfully dealing with this issue.

Step #6:   Return to reality feeling surer of yourself--knowing that you have a plan and that you can overcome this problem.

Step #7:   Take the first opportunity to use your new script. Check how strong your tendency is to go back to the old script.

Step #8    Repeat going to your Inner Sanctum and practicing your new successful scenario as needed.

**Individual Activity**

Identify one situation where you know you need to make a change. Follow the steps and write out a script that will counter the problem.

Note: You can use this method in Your Inner Sanctum where you place the image of you handling the situation exactly as you want it to be handled on your screen.

# The Three Step Technique

The three-step technique is designed for situations where you lack the time or energy to prepare a longer script or where a simple assertive technique won't do enough. This assertive technique can be shortened to three basic statements.

**Step One: I think!** Describe the situation as you see it. Make sure that you are non-blaming, and present a factually based description of the situation.

**Step Two: I feel!** Communicate your feelings about the situation using "I statements". Avoid, when possible, implying that you're holding the other person responsible for your feelings.

**Step Three: I want!** State what you want or need. Be very specific and behavioral.

EXAMPLE: A COUPLE HAVE BEEN DILIGENTLY CLEANING THEIR GARAGE OUT!

Step One: "We have been working every night for over a week to get this garage cleaned up."

Step Two: "I feel tired, uptight and stressed because I haven't had a break."

Step Three: "I would like us to start taking one night off for each three nights that we work on the garage starting tonight."

# The Three Step Technique
## Worksheet

The three step technique is designed for situations where you lack the time or energy to prepare a longer script or where a simple assertive technique won't do enough. This assertive technique can be shortened to three basic statements. Using a personal situation write out a three step assertive technique for something that is causing you distress or problems. Do two if you like.

**Scenario One:**

Step One: I think!

Step Two: I feel!

Step Three: I want!

**Scenario Two:**

Step One: I think!

Step Two: I feel!

Step Three: I want!

A copy of this form is in the appendices.

# Do's and Don'ts for Assertive Behavior

There are several do's and don'ts that you need to be aware of when you are trying to communicate assertively. The list below gives you a good sampling of some of the important things you should consider. Put a check next to areas that you personally need to work on.

## Do's

\_\_\_Learn your Assertive Techniques
\_\_\_Learn Your Script
\_\_\_Stand up straight, but not rigid.
\_\_\_Maintain a strong voice.
\_\_\_Maintain eye contact.
\_\_\_Breathe deeply and slowly.
\_\_\_Speak with good articulation.
\_\_\_Dress well, but for the occasion.
\_\_\_Practice your script or assertive technique in front of a mirror.
\_\_\_Practice your script or assertive technique in the inner Sanctum.
\_\_\_Take a deep breath and stay calm.

## Don'ts

\_\_\_Avoid Eye Contact!
\_\_\_Stare/blink or look around a lot.
\_\_\_Slouch or lean on anything.
\_\_\_Pace or walk around!
\_\_\_Wrinkle your forehead.
\_\_\_Wet your lips a lot.
\_\_\_Let your voice shake.
\_\_\_Rush your script or technique.
\_\_\_Be tight lipped.
\_\_\_Cover your mouth when talking.

# BOUNDARIES

## Section Three

This section of the workbook describes what boundaries are and what you must do to develop and then maintain them. Along with assertiveness, boundaries are essential if you are to have ongoing mental health. A person without boundaries is a person who is rarely, if ever, happy and fulfilled in life. Let's look and see how boundaries work in our lives and what we must do to further develop them. The contents of this section are:

- Boundaries — 63
- You May Need to Set Boundaries if — 65
- Two Great Boundary Killers — 66
- Boundary Weaknesses and Your Personal Code — 68
- Preliminary Guidelines to Boundary Setting — 76
- Guidelines for Boundary Setting — 77
- Boundary Truisms — 78
- Boundaries and Responsibility — 79
- Prepare for Boundary Violations — 80
- Minimize Unhealthy Relationships — 82
- Five Boundary Areas — 84
- Self-Image Model and Boundaries — 85
- Self-Image Review and Handout — 86
  - How Mental Boundaries are Damaged — 88
  - Setting Healthy Mental Boundaries — 89
  - How Social Boundaries are Damaged — 90

- Setting Healthy Social Boundaries — 91
- How Physical Boundaries are Damaged — 92
- Setting Healthy Physical Boundaries — 93
- How Spiritual Boundaries are Damaged — 94
- Setting Healthy Spiritual Boundaries — 96
- Feelings and Boundaries — 97
- Boundaries and Self — 98
- Boundaries and Personal Relationships — 99
- Boundaries and My Family — 100
- Boundaries and Friends — 101
- Boundaries and Work Situations — 102
- Personal Boundaries — 103
- My Boundaries Worksheet — 104
- Boundary Weaknesses and Your Personal Code — 105
- Other-Oriented Overt Control and Boundary Damage — 106
- Other-Oriented Overt Control and Boundary Damage Worksheet — 108
- Other-Oriented Covert Control and Boundary Damage — 109
- Other-Oriented Covert Control and Boundary Damage Worksheet — 111
- Self-Oriented Overt Control and Boundary Damage — 112
- Self-Oriented Overt Control and Boundary Damage Worksheet — 114
- Self-Oriented Covert Control and Boundary Damage — 115
- Self-Oriented Overt Control and Boundary Damage Worksheet — 118
- Reducing Self-Oriented Control Issues — 119
- Common Yet Effective Boundary Statements — 121
- Boundary Consequences and Considerations — 122
- When Boundaries Don't Work — 123

# Boundaries

Personal boundaries are guidelines, rules or limits that a person creates to identify reasonable, safe and permissible ways for other people to behave towards them and how they will respond when someone passes those limits. are the physical, emotional and mental limits we establish to protect ourselves from being manipulated, used, or violated by others. They allow us to separate who we are, and what we think and feel, from the thoughts and feelings of others. Their presence helps us express ourselves as the unique individuals we are, while we acknowledge the same in others. There are three basic types of boundaries.

- Porous Boundaries
- Rigid Boundaries
- Healthy Boundaries

### Porous Boundaries

Porous boundaries are very weak and rarely stand up to any kind of pressure. Porous boundaries are so weak that they might as well not exist. You may set the boundary, but you rarely stand up for it when needed. Others know this and simply ignore your 'boundary', knowing that nothing will happen if they breach it.

### Rigid or Inflexible Boundaries

Rigid or /Inflexible boundaries are so established that no one can get close to you either physically or emotionally. It's like you have put a solid wall around you that no one can get through. You protect yourself at all costs. This is often occurs when you have been hurt by others and finally decide to make sure that it never happens again.

### Flexible or Healthy Boundaries

Flexible or Healthy boundaries effectively protect the person who has them. The person chooses what to let in and what to keep out on a situation-specific, case-by-case basis. People with flexible, healthy boundaries are difficult to manipulate or exploit, and form the foundation of healthy relationships.

**Personal Thoughts**

Look at the boundary types listed above and do the short exercise below.

Instructions:

Write down the boundary type you predominantly use next to each of the four basic relationship areas shown below.  Is it porous, rigid or flexible?

| Relationship Boundary Areas | Type of Boundary |
|---|---|
| Personal Significant Relationship | |
| Family | |
| Friends | |
| Work Relationships | |
| | |

# You May Need to Set Healthy Boundaries If

Do you need to start setting healthy boundaries? If you aren't sure read the following. Here are some examples of when boundaries are helpful. Keep in mind that these are just a few examples of how others can take advantage of you. Check any of the below that you believe you are experiencing or have experienced with certain people in your life.

\_\_\_I feel like I am constantly having to save people and/or fix their problems.

\_\_\_I seem to be pulled into unnecessary bickering, debating and fighting often.
\_\_\_I really don't like drama, but seem to be pulled into it often.

\_\_\_People take advantage of my kindness for their own gain.

\_\_\_I spend a lot of time defending myself for things that are really not my fault (even though sometimes I am told it is my fault).
\_\_\_I am usually more invested or attracted to the person I am dating than I should be for the amount of time I have known them.
\_\_\_It seems like people I spend time with tempt me and convince me to do things that go against my desires, beliefs or values.
\_\_\_I often seem to give in to the wants and desires of other people, e.g., where to eat, stay home or go somewhere.
\_\_\_My relationship is either amazing or horrible. There doesn't seem to be an in between.
\_\_\_Every few months we break up and then work things out.

\_\_\_If the person I am dating (or married to) periodically sees someone else, I get upset but often forgive him or her.


If you checked any of the above you may very well have weak, unhealthy or non-existent boundaries. The remainder of this section will provide information about what a boundary is, how to set one up and how to establish boundary breach consequences that will make life much less chaotic.

# Two Great Boundary Killers

There are two boundary killers that plague our society today. As a group describe each of the following and how you feel that they destroy boundaries or keep you from setting them.

## Enmeshment and Boundaries

Enmeshment describes a relationship where there is a lack of clarity about where one person begins and the other ends. It is a blurring of boundaries between people. Their personal boundaries are permeable and unclear.

### Some Signs of Enmeshment

- Occurs when you feel like you need to rescue another person from their emotions.
- Occurs when you have don't have appropriate privacy between you and others.
- Occurs when your emotions and the emotions of someone else become so entwined that you cannot not tell whose emotion you are experiencing.
- Occurs when you feel like you need another person to rescue you from your own emotions.
- Occurs when you and another person are so connected that you don't have any personal emotional time and space.

Does this cause you problems? If so, highlight the signs that you exhibit and determine what you could do to address each of those issues below.

# Isolation or Avoidance and Boundaries

Social isolation can best be described as the significant reduction or absence of social contact. This occurs when you cut yourself off from normal social networks. Sometimes certain people are cut off because of conflict. Fear of conflict may drive you to isolate. When you always lose in confrontations it becomes easier and easier to Isolate or avoid others. Especial others who you know cause you conflict or who controls you. As this occurs you may have developed a multitude of avoidant strategies. You may have learned how to distract, change topics, develop ques to quickly and easily leave a room, etc. You do this so you don't have to address the conflict.

## Some Signs of Isolationism and Avoidance

- Occurs when you would rather stay home than face strangers.
- The thought of interacting with other people produces anxiety in you.
- You create reasons so that you can be alone or only be around 'safe' people.
- You learn how to change topics to avoid conflict.
- You minimize or get rid of your social media because it puts you at risk for conflict.
- You know if you have a conflict you will probably lose so you just don't put yourself in such situations.
- You develop distraction skills that keep you from having to deal with the problem or topic you are faced with.
- You avoid going anywhere you might have a conflict.
- You develop coping strategies that allow you to leave a room, situation, etc. so that you don't have to deal with conflict.
- You avoid being around anyone who has created conflict for you in the past.

If you took the Coping Styles Assessment and the last letter of your code is an 'A', you use avoidance to deal with pain, conflict, etc. You will learn to use many if not all of the above mentioned coping strategies to avoid dealing with anything uncomfortable.

# Boundary Weaknesses and Your Personal Code

If you have not taken the Coping Styles Assessment in the appendices, this information will not make sense to you. You need to identify your code so that you can look at how your code leads to certain types of boundary issues. Each of the different personal codes has a specific type of unhealthy boundary weakness. If you want to know what boundary definition is most like you, you must look at your code and identify the last three letters. That is your boundary code. For instance, if you had the code HBOA, your boundary code would be BOA. You can also look at the other codes to see how a person with that code might negatively impact you.

**My Boundary Code is:** _____

## BOUNDARY TYPES

There are three different dysfunctional boundary types that we will look at. Each type can cause significant problems for you as you relate with others. The self-oriented boundary type is extremely rigid and often aggressive. This boundary is not just protective, for it becomes a weapon to attack with for many self-oriented people. The other-oriented boundary type is extremely weak or Porous. It is defined and 'visible' yet the minute it is touched it dissolves and the individual has no protection at all. The avoidant-oriented boundary is flexible in an unhealthy way, and certainly not stable. When a person 'bumps' against someone with this type of boundary, movement immediately occurs. The person moves away from (avoids) the conflict rather than dealing with it. Each of these unhealthy boundary types can cause significant difficulties by themselves. However, when they are combined, they can cause the person to have even more complex problems. Let's see how each of these combined codes can identify serious boundary conflicts for self and others.

### Bipolar Codependency

This is a term identified by this author to describe conflicting codependencies. Specifically, when a person has both control issues and guilt or shame issues, it often places the individual on an emotional rollercoaster. Because of his self-orientation, this person desires to take charge and manipulate others to do what he wants. However, he is also other-oriented and has guilt and shame within. When he hurts someone, he feels guilty and must find a way to fix the problem. When he fixes the people problem, by saying and doing whatever it takes so that the person will 'like' him again, he is temporarily relieved. However, he gradually becomes agitated because he wants to control again. Ultimately, he takes action again to regain control. He believes that his way is better, that he should be making the decisions, and will manipulate to get what he wants if necessary. Thus, the rollercoaster begins, and the pattern continues over and over. That's why the term Bipolar Codependency was coined. It has nothing to do with Bipolar Disorder which is a biochemical issue. If you see a B at the beginning of your boundary code it simply means that you have both Self-Oriented and Other-Oriented codependency issues. The following is a list of the different personal codes and a brief definition of the boundary style that is inherent with that particular code type.

## BOA BOUNDARY STYLE

This code suggests Bipolar Codependency issues where your greatest tendency is to be other-oriented. Your boundaries flip flop between rigid and non-existent or porous. This specific code suggests that you will exhibit three unhealthy boundary types—other-oriented or porous, self-oriented or rigid and avoidant. In most cases boundaries are Initially weak or porous if even present. As a result, you are easily hurt by others. However, at times you put up a strong boundary and actually breach other people's established boundaries to get your way. This occurs when your self-oriented boundary style takes hold and either becomes a wall of protection or it turns into a weapon that can be used to run over or take control of others. However, due to the bipolarity of this code, when the wall is put up or when the it becomes a weapon that hurts others, you eventually feel guilty. The "A" in the code suggests that there will be times that an avoidance will be used. When in conflict and you know you are in a losing situation, you may withdraw if possible and simply not deal with a conflict (unless the self-oriented part of you communicates that the conflict can be won).

### Damage to Self

This boundary style suggests that you are indecisive, confused and frustrated. Self-Esteem is either superficially high or extremely low. Self-Identity is weak or non-existent because of the issues that produce this dysfunctional boundary type. Foundational values are often weak and/or are everchanging to meet your personal desires or to please others. You may feeling like you are on an emotional rollercoaster.

### Damage to Others

This boundary style produces discomfort in others. People find you hard to read due to your switching roles and as a result they would prefer to not be around you, especially when you are controlling. Others, who are controlling in nature may be drawn to you so that they can control you. However, this often produces ongoing conflict. Some people feel frustrated because they can't get a straight answer when there is a conflict. When you know you are in a losing situation you will avoid dealing with the conflict, which causes the other person to be angry and upset.

### BON BOUNDARY STYLE

This code suggests Bipolar Codependency issues where your greatest tendency is to be other-oriented. Your boundaries flip flop between rigid and non-existent or porous. This specific code suggests that you will exhibit three unhealthy boundary types—other-oriented or porous, self-oriented or rigid and avoidant. In most cases boundaries are Initially weak or porous if even present. As a result, you are easily hurt by others. However, at times you put up a strong boundary and actually breach other people's established boundaries to get your way. This occurs when your self-oriented boundary style takes hold and either becomes a wall of protection or it turns into a weapon that can be used to run over or take control of others. However, due to the bipolarity of this code, when the wall is put up or when the it becomes a weapon that hurts others, you eventually feel guilty. The "N" in the code suggests that you will rarely avoid conflict. Avoidance is non-existent as a boundary. As a result, you will usually deal with conflict head on. You may lose or will periodically win by controlling others to get your way only to feel guilty later.

## Damage to Self

This boundary style promotes indecisiveness, confusion and frustration. There is no avoidance so you face conflict head on and inevitably takes on pain whenever there is a conflict. It also causes you to experience the rollercoaster effect emotionally.

## Damage to Others

The indecisiveness causes confusion for others who deal with this boundary style. People know that they can take advantage of you. The temptation is often strong. Those who have controlling tendencies will find ways to control your life, while at the same time damaging themselves. However, at times you will get tired of being controlled and will take a stand. This produces conflict for those who are attempting to control you.

## UOA BOUNDARY STYLE

This means you are experiencing unipolar boundary issues, which are specifically other-oriented in nature. Your boundaries are very porous or non-existent. A boundary style like this promotes two unhealthy boundary types--other and avoidant. You really have no boundaries and sadly others often take advantage of you. You have one way out. If things get too painful, you will find ways to avoid the conflict. However, this just postpones the pain.

## Damage to Self

Personal needs are suppressed to make sure that others are taken care of in some way. Self is usually put aside until problems are resolved. You will often feel like you are being devalued. Self-Esteem is weak and you may often feel depressed, hopeless and overwhelmed. There is often mental and physical exhaustion. Your avoidance makes it even more difficult to protect yourself by resolving problems. It's much too easy to simply avoid…..when you can. When you have this code you are practically asking for someone to control you.

### Damage to Others

Contributes to the development of controlling in other people. It supports the controlling nature of controllers.

### UON BOUNDARY STYLE

This means you are experiencing unipolar boundary issues, which are specifically other-oriented in nature. Your boundaries are very porous or non-existent. A boundary style like this promotes two unhealthy boundary types--other and avoidant. You really have no boundaries and sadly others often take advantage of you. You have no way out.

### Damage to Self

This means that you are constantly worn out emotionally and physically. With no boundaries and no avoidant mechanisms you are constantly set up by self and others to take on burdens of others. There is no self-identity. Personal needs are suppressed to make sure that others are taken care of in some way. Self is usually put aside until problems are resolved. This is an extreme case where self-esteem is very weak. You will often feel depressed, overwhelmed and hopeless. When you have this code you are practically asking for someone to control you and you have no avoidance mechanisms to 'protect you'.

### Damage to Others

Can promote control in others who really don't want it. It supports the controlling nature of controllers.

### BSA BOUNDARY STYLE

This means you are experiencing Bipolar Codependency issues that are predominantly self-oriented in nature. As a result, the boundaries flip flop between rigid and non-existent. This boundary style exhibits all three unhealthy boundary types--self, other and avoidant Most of the time the boundaries are very rigid. These rigid boundaries come across as control and sometimes hostility. However, in certain circumstances or with certain people, few if any boundaries are evident. There are times when you will let someone slip through and cause pain. When possible, you will find some way to avoid conflict unless you know that you can get your way. When you can't get your way overtly, you may become passive aggressive.

**Damage to Self**

Distances others unless they need you, because of your rigid boundaries, and destructive control issues. Your control often offends others and drives them away, so isolation and loneliness are sometimes present. There are times when this code type will open itself up to pain when you are using your shame-based boundary type.

**Damage to Others**

Often critical, harsh and demeaning. Wants to be in control and will cause pain or problems for others if they don't comply. Constantly attacking others which causes them to not want to be around you. You will often hurt others which in turn causes them pain.

## BSN BOUNDARY STYLE

This means you are experiencing Bipolar Codependency issues that are predominantly self-oriented in nature. No avoidance is noted in this style. As a result, the boundaries flip flop between rigid and non-existent. This boundary style exhibits no avoidance. Most of the time the boundaries are very rigid. These rigid boundaries come across as control and sometimes hostility. However, in certain circumstances or with certain people, few if any boundaries are evident. There are times when you will let someone slip through and cause pain. When you can't get your way overtly, you may become passive aggressive. When there is conflict, you will face the problem head on instead of avoiding.

**Damage to Self**

Distances others unless they need you, because of your rigid boundaries, and destructive control issues. Your control often offends others and drives them away, so isolation and loneliness are sometimes present. There are times when this code type will open itself up to pain when you are using your shame-based boundary type. You may find it hard to be tactful.

## Damage to Others

People with this boundary code will most often cause others to feel guilty. The control seems to push people into a shame state. Constantly attacking others which causes them to not want to be around you. You will often hurt others which in turn causes them pain.

## USA BOUNDARY STYLE

This means you are experiencing unipolar boundary issues, which are specifically self-oriented in nature. It also suggests that you use avoidance. Most of the time your boundaries are very rigid. You are probably very rigid and controlling. Your boundaries are firm and do not allow for exceptions. When you experience conflict, you will usually win and will walk all over people who are in your way. These rigid boundaries come across as control and sometimes hostility. When possible, you will find some way to avoid conflict unless you know that you can get your way. When you can't get your way overtly, you may become passive aggressive.

## Damage to Self

No friends and poor relationships are common-place. Produces loneliness! Your controlling attitude and actions will keep people distanced or unhappy with you.

## Damage to Others

Others are often hurt by your controlling and sometimes manipulative attacks that are either direct or indirect. Damage to self-esteem, inability to function well socially, educationally or at work often occurs. People are seen as a means to an end and they know it.

## USN BOUNDARY STYLE

This means you are experiencing unipolar boundary issues, which are specifically self-oriented in nature. It also suggests that you do not use avoidance. This boundary style exhibits one unhealthy boundary type-self. This code type is the most inflexible of all. Totally controlling this boundary type will bulldoze over everyone in its path. People who use this code type will always meet problems head on and keep going no matter who or what is in the way. They rarely lose! If they do, everyone around them becomes miserable.

### Damage to Self

No friends and poor relationships are common-place. Produces loneliness! Your controlling attitude and actions will keep people distanced or unhappy with you.

### Damage to Others

Others are often hurt by your controlling and sometimes manipulative attacks that are either direct or indirect. Damage to self-esteem, inability to function well socially, educationally or at work often occurs. People are seen as a means to an end and they know it.

Each one of these boundary types cause significant damage to everyone involved. Look closely at your boundary type to see how much damage you are causing self and others. It is by recognition first that you can produce change. Now that you are beginning to see how your boundaries can be breached or how you may be breaching other people boundaries. Let's look at the areas that you need to consider as you start to develop boundaries for yourself and honor the boundaries of others. Each of these areas are extremely important to your emotional well-being and healthy boundaries must be established if you are to lead a healthy, happy life.

# Preliminary Guidelines to Boundary Setting

Life without boundaries is no life at all. However, some people, for whatever reason, are not willing to do what it takes to set boundaries so they can truly live life. If you really want to 'have a life' you must set boundaries. The first thing that must be present is desire. If you don't really want to set boundaries so that you can lead a healthy life, it will never happen. Here are some preliminary guidelines that should be considered before you begin to set boundaries.

1. The dominant force behind boundary setting is a desire to set and maintain them. Without desire, healthy boundaries cannot exist.

2. Determine what you are getting as a result of your lack of boundaries and what you may lose when you set them.

3. Once you have defined your possible loss, you must decide if you're willing to risk what you may lose.

4. You must be willing to enforce the consequences that occur as a result of your boundary or it may be better to simply not set them.

5. When you do lose something, do what you must to make up for the loss if it is important to you.

6. Establishing the boundary is the beginning, not the end. Now you must battle others who resist your boundaries. Get strength from those who care and/or support you.

7. Don't let your resistance keep you from doing what is best for you!

# Guidelines for Boundary Setting

Now that you have looked closely at some of the preliminary guidelines that must be considered, it's time for you to understand what must be done to set healthy boundaries. There are several guidelines, that when followed, will help you set healthy boundaries. This is not a complete list of guidelines; however, if you check yourself with this list, you may avoid some problems that have occurred with others who have tried to establish healthy boundaries.

1. When you begin, set small boundaries with people you trust to assure success. Don't try to set major boundaries at first unless it's essential to your health and safety.
2. Boundaries can be set only when you are ready, and not a minute sooner. Just because someone tells you that you need boundaries doesn't mean that you are ready to set them. When you are ready, get serious about setting boundaries then do it.
3. Look at all your relationships and determine how others may be taking advantage of you (or possibly how you are taking advantage of others). Identify problem situations and then clearly set a limit that will protect you and others.
4. When you set boundaries, be specific, non-emotional and use as few words as possible.
5. Boundaries are not rigid and unchanging. They must be flexible and dynamic, yet strong enough to protect you.
6. You can know that when you set a boundary people around you will test it to see if you're serious about that specific boundary. Controllers will try to demolish it either overtly or covertly. Be ready!
7. Only you can define what you are comfortable with, so your boundaries should be very personal, not just a set of rules or limits someone else has established.
8. Healthy boundaries must include reasonable risk and trust.
9. Boundaries must have consequences, or they are not real boundaries.
10. Boundaries should not compromise your belief system or values. They should support them.

# Boundary Truisms

There are several truisms and sometimes just simple common sense that can help you maintain your boundaries. Look at each of the statements below and determine if they are true for you.

1. Boundaries only work when you are prepared and able to take action to maintain your boundaries when 'under fire'.
2. Boundaries are weak if you allow others to determine your feelings and/or thoughts. You have the right to determine what thoughts you have in your head. No one else has a right to 'force' you to think in a way that is unacceptable to you.
3. Walls are not boundaries! Boundaries are not intended to be rigid and unmovable--they must be flexible to be healthy.
4. Regardless of 'who' is responsible for a thought, you must take the consequences, good or bad, for what you think.
5. If you are shame based, you will probably feel ashamed and afraid when you set boundaries.
6. You must have the necessary tools to stand up for your boundaries, provide consequences when necessary or assertively protect yourself when needed.
7. Make sure that you have a good support system that can validate you and the boundaries you set.
8. Spend time with people who respect your boundaries.
9. Don't spend time with people who consistently try to break down, damage or alter your boundaries in any way without your thoughtful permission.
10. Rigid or powerful boundaries that are used to try to 'hurt' others are not healthy boundaries. They become mechanisms for attacking others.
11. Boundaries without consequences are not boundaries.
12. It is not possible to simultaneously set a boundary and take care of another person's feelings.

# Boundaries and Responsibility

Boundaries are one of the most important elements in developing a healthy self-identity. However, we must understand that boundaries should not become a way for us to isolate from others and their needs. When you begin to develop boundaries, you must start to accept the responsibilities that go along with them. The following statements suggest what responsibilities we have when it comes to others and what it means to be responsible to others.

1. You're responsible to others, but not for them.

2. This means that we can show our love and compassion to others by helping them when they have problems that are too great for them to handle on their own.

3. We all have responsibilities that we must carry on our own. However, there are times when the load is obviously impossible for one person to carry.

4. It is our responsibility to aid others in times of crisis or pain. This does not mean that we take on their responsibility; it means that we help them with their responsibility.


Motivation: Love, Mercy, Compassion


NOT: People Pleasing, Caretaking, Approval Seeking

> *If you take responsibility and fix another person's problem you are enabling him, not helping him.*
> *Or*
> *If you give a man a fish he will eat for a day, if you teach him how to fish he will eat for a lifetime.*

# Prepare for Boundary Violations

Even when you establish good boundaries, it doesn't mean that someone will not try to violate them. It is very important that you understand that people will test or try to break down your boundaries. Your job is to 1) establish boundaries that protect you, 2) watch for situations where someone may try to test or break down your boundaries, and 3) develop a plan for addressing such attacks. Obviously, there are a multitude of different situations where someone can attempt to test or break down your boundaries. Let's look at a few of these.

- What would you do in a work setting if your boss wanted you to stay late on a consistent basis (no pay included)?
- What would you do if your boss sent an e-mail Saturday saying he needs you do a work-related activity on Sunday?
- What would you do if a friend needed to borrow your lawn mower again because he doesn't want to buy one?
- What would you do if your partner kept taking cash out of a secret place you put cash for an emergency?

The point of this is that you must be prepared for how you will address boundary violations. Here are some suggestions.

1. Watch and be prepared for boundary violations that seem to consistently happen! Is it a particular person who does this? If so, is that person important in your life or can you minimize your contact?
2. If you have specific boundary violations that occur often by particular people you may want to develop an assertive response that helps you stand up for your boundary. Identify the Assertive skill you want to use, build a statement that specifically addresses that boundary violation and practice it in your mind. You can also go to the Inner Sanctum and practice it on your screen.
3. When someone attempts to violate your boundary and you are not prepared you may want to use the Assertive Delay Technique. Simply put them off, say you can't make that decision right now, and walk away.

4. If your work environment is completely toxic and you believe it will not get better, it may be time to get a new job. Always get your job before you quit.
5. If you are in a toxic personal relationship with someone and they constantly violate your boundaries after you have explained to them that is causing problems, you may have to back off of the relationship or discontinue it. Remember, you can't change someone. Each person must be able to change himself.
6. If a 'friend' is toxic and consistently violates your boundaries you may need to minimize that relationship or discontinue it.

There is one thing that you can choose to control that will help you reduce boundary violations significantly.

> *Carefully choose who you spend time with, who you build relationship with. Who you choose to spend time with will either help you become a better version of yourself, or a worse version of yourself.*

With this in mind let's look at how you might do that in your daily life.

# Minimize Unhealthy Relationships

Who you spend time with often impacts on your character. Who you spend time with can determine the amount of stress you have in your life and how often boundaries are tested or violated. Who you spend time with can either reduce or increase lost time depending on the responsibility of the individual's behavior. Who you spend time with can either improve your quality of life (this includes your partner if you have one), or it can cause damage or problems. With this in mind, it is important to spend time with people who are:

- Trustworthy!
- share similar values!
- Fun loving and share some common interests!
- Enjoy some of the same fun activities!
- Very dependable and trustworthy!
- Don't test or violate your boundaries.

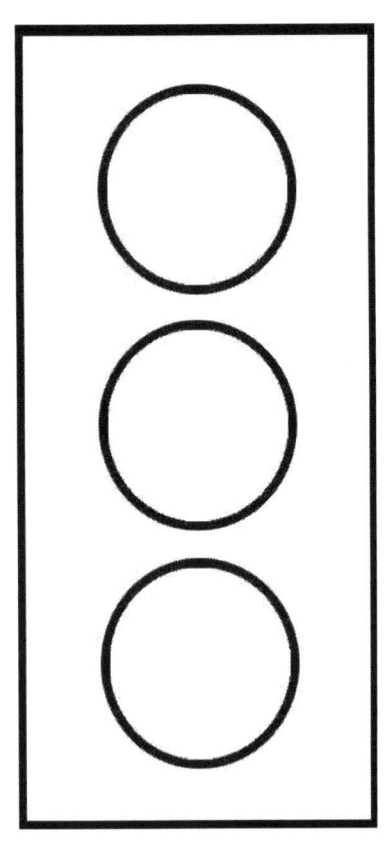

**Green People**
   Trustworthy even with bigger things
   Share common Interests and values
   Dependable
   Rarely if ever test or violate your boundaries

**Yellow People**
   Trustworthy with smaller things
   Share some common interests or values
   Dependable at times
   May test or violate boundaries

**Red People**
   Not very trustworthy if at all
   Shares few if any common interests or values
   Not very dependable
   Tests and Violates boundaries often

## Protecting Yourself from Unhealthy Relationships

**Red:** Red people are people who do not share the same values, beliefs, etc. that you have. You may meet a person who does things that are totally opposite of what you believe, who does not appear to be healthy at all, e.g., untreated alcoholism, drug addict, physical abuser, someone who financially irresponsible, who won't hold down a job, sexual abuser. Such people will often test or violate your boundaries. NOTE: We all want to help people when they are 'red' and we should. However, your focus should be on an attempt to relate with him in a way that will lead him out of the red. Only you can determine if the time spend is damaging to you and yours, or if it is truly being beneficial to him. It's a hard call, but it's one you must make.

**Yellow:** Unless a person you meet is obviously red when you meet him it is a very high probability that everyone you meet will be yellow. Why yellow? Yellow people don't appear be 'bad', nor do you know them well enough to put your complete trust, faith, etc. in them initially. When you meet a yellow person, he might be courteous, kind, thoughtful, etc. However, it is ONLY with time that you can determine what he is really like inside. You wouldn't trust a stranger, even if he was nice, to watch your purse while you ran to get a half-gallon of milk from the back of the store. This is very important! Trust is gained and grows as the person shows that he is trustworthy. This is also important! You start with small things to develop trust, not big things (like your purse in a shopping cart). As a person shows that he is trustworthy in small things, you graduate to bigger, bigger and bigger things until you can have a high level of trust in that person. Sometimes a person stays yellow. He isn't completely dependable, trustworthy and periodically tests or violates your boundaries.

> *Surround yourself with Green People. They will rarely let you down, or seek to test or violate your boundaries.*

When you do this, you will find that your life has less conflict and frustration.

For more information about this concept see the Foundations Workbook by this author.

# Five Boundary Areas

There are five basic boundary area that you must be able to protect and care for if you are to become and stay a healthy individual.

## INTERNAL BOUNDARIES

There are three basic internal boundaries that we must consider as we define how to care for ourselves. They are:

- Mental Boundaries
- Spiritual Boundaries
- Feeling Boundaries

## EXTERNAL BOUNDARIES

There are two basic external boundaries that we must consider as we learn how to care for our external self. They are:

- Social Boundaries
- Physical Boundaries

# Self-Image Model and Boundaries

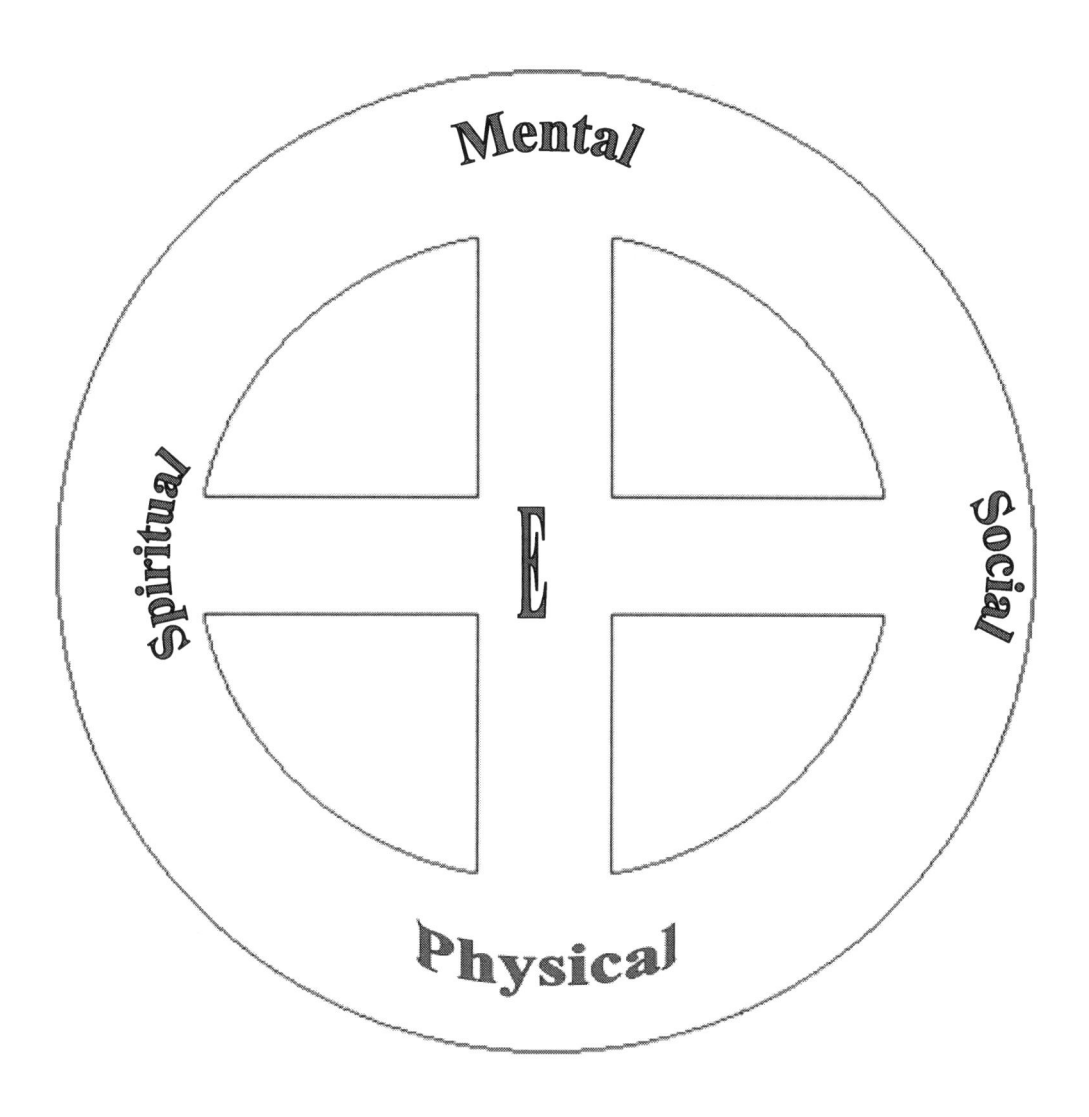

Mental

Spiritual

E

Social

Physical

> *"No one can make you feel inferior without your consent."*
> *Eleanor Roosevelt*

# Self-Image

### Review and Handout

This self-image model addresses four specific areas for the individual. Each area is critical for personal and relationship health. If you are experiencing any boundary violations it can produce constant frustration as well as physical and emotional stress.

**Mental Self**

Your mental self consists of all that you think. The sad thing is that much of what you think can be unhealthy and lead you to thoughts, words and actions that can be negative or damaging to yourself and others. If you are experiencing cognitive distortions or negative thoughts of any kind it can lead to negative emotions. Positive emotions are often the result of positive, healthy thinking that leads to a healthier life.

| Healthy | Unhealthy |
| --- | --- |
| Optimistic | Pessimistic |
| Positive Mental Tapes | Negative Mental Tapes |
| Goal Oriented | Cognitive Distortions |
|  |  |

**Social Self**

The social self has to do with whether you have people in your life who are close to you, people who you can talk to, have fun with. If you don't have such people you feel isolated, alone If you don't have this you will have a tendency to isolate, be unhappy, stagnate. This produces unwanted, unhealthy feelings.

| Healthy | Unhealthy |
| --- | --- |
| A close friend | People who are untrustworthy |
| Healthy Social Group | People who are not dependable |
| Ongoing Fun with others | People who do not share values |
| Time with others for growth purposes | People who bring you down |

## Physical Self

The physical self includes multiple areas; weight, clothes, hygiene, hair, toning/muscle, internal physical health, and how your body is responding to stress. If you haven't done the best you can with what you have, it will cause you to be embarrassed, unsure, keep you from socializing, cause you to think unhealthy thoughts, etc. This is why it is important that we all do all that we can to look our best and take care of our bodies if we are to be as healthy as we would like. If we don't, it produces unwanted thoughts and feelings.

| Healthy | Unhealthy |
| --- | --- |
| Proper weight | Overweight/Underweight |
| Exercise for health | Poor exercise habits |
| Hygiene, shaving, makeup, etc. | Poor hygiene, shaving, makeup, etc. |
| Clothes | Unkempt, mismatched clothes |

## Spiritual/Moral Self

The spiritual or moral self has to do with the values you hold within yourself that helps you determine right from wrong, good from bad. You cannot have good self-judgment if you do not have a strong, consistent value base. Self-Judgment occurs when you have the ability to make good decisions. It's up to you to determine what values or beliefs you hold that will help you in making daily decisions. In this workbook we will focus on some the more common values or beliefs that help us build a good foundation.

| Healthy | Unhealthy |
| --- | --- |
| Good Self-Judgment/Discipline | Poor Self-Judgment/Discipline |
| Good Self-Discipline | Poor Self-Discipline |
| Known core beliefs/values | Situational values or beliefs |
| Beliefs/Values key in decision making | Personal wants, needs, desires are key in decision making |

# How Mental Boundaries are Damaged

Read each of the ways that your mental boundaries can be damaged or destroyed. Put a check next to any that you personally use or that happens to you.

**Self-Imposed Damage**

_____Magnification: Making things worse than they really are!

_____Minimization: Making things out to be less a problem than they really are!

_____Rationalization: Finding a way to justify that what you have done (what has happened, etc.) is all right when it really isn't.

_____Denial: Stating that there is no problem when it is evident to everyone else that there really is a problem.

_____Codependent thinking, negative tapes or cognitive distortions.

_____Not allowing yourself to use your mental ability or knowledge due to fears, anxiety, etc.

_____Telling yourself that you are stupid, not capable, etc.

**Other-Imposed Damage**

_____Not giving you information that you need or giving you poor information.

_____Giving you too much information, too fast, too early.

_____Situations where you are not allowed to have private thoughts.

_____Situations where you are expected to perform at an expected intellectual level.

_____Not being allowed to question information or clarify things as they occur.

_____Not giving you opportunity to stimulate yourself intellectually.

# Setting Healthy Mental Boundaries

Here are a few boundaries that you can consider as you seek to develop healthy boundaries for your personal life. Look at these different boundaries and how they protect particular parts of you. Adapt them to your own personal needs. Remember, each of these boundaries must have a consequence or it's not really a boundary.

**Healthy Mental Boundaries**

Here are some examples of healthy mental boundaries. This is not intended to be a complete listing. It is merely a short list to give you examples of how you would set a mental boundary.

- I am not responsible for your feelings or emotions!

    Consequence:

- I am responsible for my own feelings or emotions!

    Consequence:

- I am not responsible for your actions!

    Consequence:

- I have a right to learn--it's okay to seek information and learn.

    Consequence:

- I am not responsible for your thoughts!

    Consequence:

# How Social Boundaries are Damaged

Read each of the ways that your mental boundaries can be damaged or destroyed. Put a check next to any that you personally use or that happens to you.

**Self-Imposed Damage**

_____When you allow people to tell you what to think, they are breaching your boundaries.

_____When people tell you what you really mean when you have said what you mean.

_____When you allow others to speak for you without your permission.

_____When you allow people to improve or change your thoughts.

_____When you let someone determine what your interests are without your input.

_____When you let people lead you into their interests instead of following your own.

**Other-Imposed Damage**

_____Being made fun of in social situations.

_____Being intentionally ignored by another person.

_____When people do not listen to you.

_____When someone calls you names, such as "stupid, crazy or lumphead".

_____When people expect you to live in a situation where there are secrets, denial of problems, etc.

_____When people do not allow you to have your feelings.

_____When others don't let you deal with your physical pain or abuse or not being protected.

# Setting Healthy Social Boundaries

Here are some examples of healthy social boundaries. This is not intended to be a complete listing. It is merely a short list to give you examples of how you would set a social boundary.

- I need to balance my time between socialization and alone time!

    Consequence:

- I have a right to make my own decisions about who I spend time with, where I go, etc. In doing so I will keep the best interests of our relationship at heart!

    Consequence:

- I do not have to listen to unproductive negative statements or rage when we communicate!

    Consequence:

- I want to hear and understand your opinions, but what I think and say are also important!

    Consequence:

- Even though I care, I cannot fix your problems; I can only fix myself!

    Consequence:

# How Physical Boundaries are Damaged

Read each of the ways that your mental boundaries can be damaged or destroyed. Put a check next to any that you personally use or that happens to you.

### Self-Imposed Damage

_____ When you intentionally hurt yourself in any way.

_____ When you take illegal drugs.

_____ When you drink to excess.

_____ When you have poor personal hygiene.

_____ When you fail to provide good nutritional foods for yourself (too much junk food). When you fail to allow physical touch by others.

_____ When you smoke.


### Other-Imposed Damage

_____ When you are hit, slapped, kicked, shoved, pushed, pinched, shook or choked.

_____ When you are physically restrained.

_____ When you are touched sexually without your permission.

_____ When someone teases or demeans you because of your body.

_____ When others expect you to maintain a certain standard of external appearance that is really a personal preference.

_____ When others shame you about your body or any of its functions.

_____ When you are around people who smoke.

# Setting Healthy Physical Boundaries

Here are some examples of healthy physical boundaries. This is not intended to be a complete listing. It is merely a short list to give you examples of how you would set a physical boundary.

- No one has the right to be sexual with me without my permission.

    Consequence:

- I can determine how physically close I want anyone else to be.

    Consequence:

- I reserve the right to decide with whom, when, and how I will be sexual.

    Consequence:

- Any person I have agreed to be sexual with may only be sexual with me in the ways I agree to.

    Consequence:

- Nobody has the right to touch me without my permission.

    Consequence:

- I reserve the right to give others permission to touch me only in ways that I want to be touched.

    Consequence:

- I reserve the right to control how, when, where and who touches me.

    Consequence:

- I can determine what is best for my body when it comes to rest, eating, etc.

    Consequence:

# How Spiritual Boundaries are Damaged

Read each of the ways that your mental boundaries can be damaged or destroyed. Put a check next to any that you personally use or that happens to you.

**Self-Imposed Damage**

_____Poor prayer life.

_____When you are religious instead of spiritual.

_____When you become overzealous to the point that it causes an imbalance in your life or another's life.
_____When your religion becomes obsessive.

_____When your religion develops an overly mystical or magical quality.

_____If you become involved with any cult.

_____If you are involved with any anti-religious groups or have anti-GOD beliefs.
_____You damage yourself when you choose to have no value system other than what feel right to you.
_____When you fail to become involved with other spiritual people who are growing spiritually.

**Other Imposed Damage**

_____Your family is extremely over-religious.

_____Your family is so involved with religion that you are isolated from the community.
_____When religion is focused on and spirituality is absent or placed in second place.
_____When your 'church' promotes excessive religious rules that 'protect' their flock.

_____When GOD is promoted as a vindictive, fearful entity.

_____When you are not given any spiritual guidance.

_____When you are not taught a sense of right and wrong.

_____When you are not allowed to challenge tradition and human interpreted theology.

_____When you are punished for having a different interpretation of theology.

_____Any guilt or fear-based religion.

_____When your church has legalistic beliefs.

_____When your parents never expose you to a healthy spirituality.

_____When your church focuses on theology and minimizes real needs or people issues.

_____When the leadership puts themselves on a pedestal and acts as if they are better even though they say they aren't.

# Setting Healthy Spiritual Boundaries

Here are some examples of healthy spiritual boundaries. This is not intended to be a complete listing. It is merely a short list to give you examples of how you would set a spiritual boundary.

- I am responsible for my own actions!

    Consequence:

- I must stand up for what I believe in or maintain my values even when you don't agree.

    Consequence:

- I must be responsible for what I believe in and how I will stand up for those beliefs. No one else can make those decisions for me.

    Consequence:

- I will go to the church of my choosing or not!

    Consequence:

- I don't have to believe everything a church leader or spiritual guide tells me.

    Consequence:

Personal Situation:

    Consequence:

# Feelings and Boundaries

Our feelings are often determined by how healthy or unhealthy our self-image is on a day by day basis. If our actions and decisions are in accordance with our self-image, then our feelings will naturally be healthy (even though they may be painful at times). Look back at page 76-78 and review the Self-Image Model and when it is not healthy how it negatively impacts you. It shows four basic areas of self-image that we all have. The interesting thing is:

- If you have a Poor Mental Self-Image it will produce negative feelings.
  - Cognitive distortions, negative tapes, codependent thinking, etc.
- If you have a Poor Social Self-Image it will produce negative feelings.
  - Poor social relationships, unhealthy relationships, isolation, etc.
- If you have a Poor Physical Self-Image it will produce negative feelings.
  - Weigh too much, weight too little, cleanliness, not doing things to enhance your positives, no exercise, stressed out, etc.
- If you have a Poor Spiritual Self-Image it will produce negative feelings.
  - No core belief system, not living up to your beliefs, feeling guilty, etc.

**Address the Cause of Unwanted Hurtful Feelings:** Your unhealthy negative feelings are a result of negative thoughts or experiences you are having in each of the four areas. That doesn't mean that someone couldn't have other issues that contribute or cause unhealthy feelings. However, the vast amount of unhealthy feelings you experience today is a result of you not experiencing a healthy sense of self in each of those four areas.

**Identify Healthy Boundaries for all Self-Image Areas:** You must address boundary issues in all the self-image areas if you are to be healthy. Previous pages address boundary issues for each of the areas of self-image. Make sure that you work through each of these areas. feel better about yourself and will be able to set protective boundaries around yourself.

See the **Foundations Workbook – Revised** by F. Russell Crites, Jr.

# Boundaries and Self

Each of these statements represent a way in which you can damage, destroy, minimize or negate your own personal boundaries. It is not always others that breach your boundaries and cause you pain; often your greatest enemy is self. Read each of the statements below a check it if you feel it is something that you often do to yourself.

_____ 1. When you use eating to avoid intimacy or healthy relationships.

_____ 2. You find yourself taking control in situations that you are uncomfortable in.

_____ 3. You have an inability to delay physical gratification.

_____ 4. You have trouble finishing tasks that you begin.

_____ 5. Time is out of control for you. You are late, miss meetings, etc. consistently.

_____ 6. Your financial income is not as great as how much you spend on a monthly basis.

_____ 7. You find that you have trouble saying, 'No' to yourself when you know you really need to.

_____ 8. When you listen to yourself, you find that you often put yourself down.

_____ 9. When you recognize that you have threatened someone (verbally, physically, sexually, etc.).

_____ 10. When you use drinking to deal with your pain or problems.

# Boundaries and Personal Relationships

Personal relationships are often where our boundaries fall short. Here are some basic statements that will help you determine if your boundaries are intact. As you read these, try to determine if you are allowing those to whom you are close to control your feelings or if you are controlling others in some way. If you are allowing others to control your feelings, then your boundaries are weak or fragile. If you are controlling other people's feelings, then your boundaries may be too rigid. If your boundaries are healthy, you will find that you are flexible and congruent. Read each of the statements below and determine if any of them are true about you most of the time. It would be true even if it was only in one relationship.

\_\_\_\_\_ 1. You will stay in a relationship that is not good for you even though you know better.

\_\_\_\_\_ 2. You find yourself controlling the one you love.

\_\_\_\_\_ 3. You have a pretty good day, but your partners bad mood ruins your day.

\_\_\_\_\_ 4. When you have a conflict with your partner, you usually leave the room rather than deal with it at the time.

\_\_\_\_\_ 5. You begin to question your own judgment when your partner disagrees with your assessment of a movie you have just watched together.

\_\_\_\_\_ 6. You give advice or tell your partner how to handle a problem when it is not asked for.

\_\_\_\_\_ 7. Your partner wants to use something that has sentimental value to you that could easily be broken and you allow it to be borrowed because you don't want your partner to be upset at you.

\_\_\_\_\_ 8. You and your partner have a disagreement, so you isolate or avoid him for a while.

\_\_\_\_\_ 9. When your partner wants to be close to you physically and you don't feel like it, you try to keep yourself busy, hide, or anything else that will postpone the situation.

\_\_\_\_\_ 10. You take things out on your partner when you don't get your way.

# Boundaries and My Family

Our family relationships are also a place where our boundaries can easily be breached. This page has some basic statements listed that will help you determine if your boundaries are intact. As you read these, try to determine if you are allowing any family members to control your feelings or if you are controlling others in some way. If you are allowing others to control your feelings, your boundaries are weak or fragile. If you are controlling other people's feelings, your boundaries may be too rigid. If your boundaries are healthy, you will find that you are flexible and congruent. Read each of the statements below and determine if any of them are true about you most of the time. It would be true even if it was only in one family relationship.

_____ 1. Physical affection is not appropriate and positive in my family.

_____ 2. Family members do not have privacy when it is wanted or needed.

_____ 3. I felt distanced from members of my family.

_____ 4. My family does not spend much time together when we have opportunity.

_____ 5. My family has a tendency to isolate; we have few real friendships with other families.

_____ 6. In my family the rules are very rigid.

_____ 7. Members of my family are not allowed to be self-reliant or independent.

_____ 8. Feelings are not discussed in my family.

_____ 9. It is rarely okay to express opinions at home.

_____ 10. Fun and laughter are considered irresponsible behavior in my family.

# Boundaries and Friends

'Friendships' are also a place where boundaries can be damaged. This page has some basic statements listed that will help you determine if your boundaries are intact with your friends. As you read these try to determine if you are allowing your friends to control your feelings or if you are controlling them in some way. If you are allowing your friends to control your feelings, then your boundaries are weak or fragile. If you are controlling your friends' feelings, then your boundaries may be too rigid. If your boundaries are healthy you will find that you are flexible and congruent. Read each of the statements below and determine if any of them are true about you most of the time. It would be true even if it was only in one relationship.

_____ 1. You will allow your friends to borrow things that you really don't want to let them take.

_____ 2. You find that it's easy to get others to do what you want most of the time.

_____ 3. You have a pretty good day, but a friend says or does something that ruins your day.

_____ 4. You have a conflict with a friend and instead of dealing with it you leave.

_____ 5. When your friend experiences some pain as a result of a life event you feel almost as bad as he does.

_____ 6. You give advice when it is not asked for.

_____ 7. A neighbor asks to borrow your lawn mower. You really don't want to loan it to him but you say, 'Yes.' anyway.

_____ 8. You and a friend have a disagreement so you avoid being around him.

_____ 9. A new acquaintance asks you to come over for dinner. You don't feel comfortable so you give a 'lame' excuse about how you can't make it.

_____ 10. You take things out on others when you don't get your way.

# Boundaries and Work Situations

Our work setting often provides situations where our boundaries can be damaged. This page has some basic statements listed that will help you determine if your boundaries are intact in your work environment. As you read these try to determine if you are allowing those you work with to have control over you or your feelings or if you are controlling them in some way. If you are allowing others to control your feelings, your boundaries are weak or fragile. If you are controlling other people's feelings, your boundaries may be too rigid. If your boundaries are healthy, you will find that you are flexible and congruent. Read each of the statements below and determine if any of them are true about you most of the time. It would be true even if it was only in one work relationship.

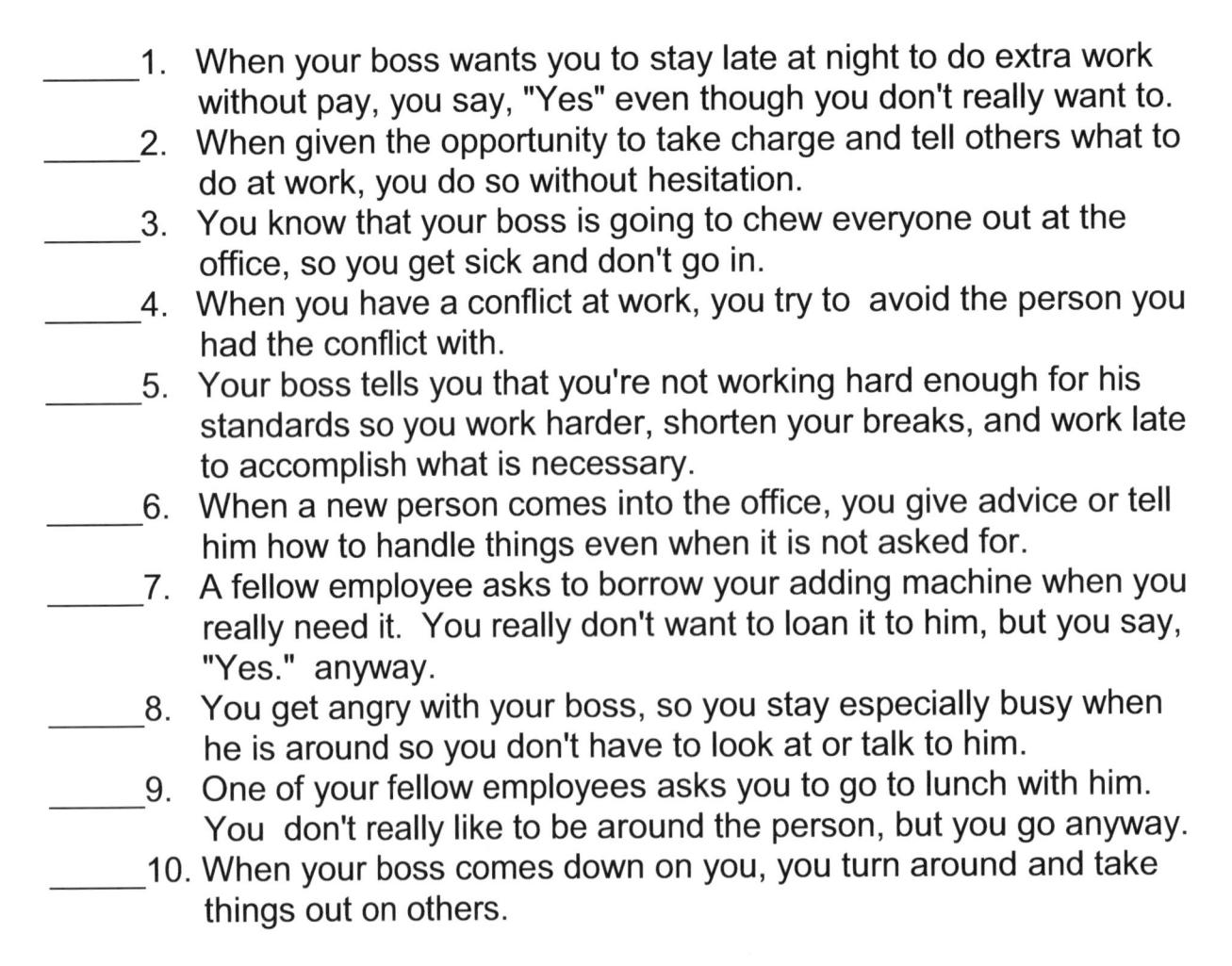

\_\_\_\_\_ 1. When your boss wants you to stay late at night to do extra work without pay, you say, "Yes" even though you don't really want to.

\_\_\_\_\_ 2. When given the opportunity to take charge and tell others what to do at work, you do so without hesitation.

\_\_\_\_\_ 3. You know that your boss is going to chew everyone out at the office, so you get sick and don't go in.

\_\_\_\_\_ 4. When you have a conflict at work, you try to avoid the person you had the conflict with.

\_\_\_\_\_ 5. Your boss tells you that you're not working hard enough for his standards so you work harder, shorten your breaks, and work late to accomplish what is necessary.

\_\_\_\_\_ 6. When a new person comes into the office, you give advice or tell him how to handle things even when it is not asked for.

\_\_\_\_\_ 7. A fellow employee asks to borrow your adding machine when you really need it. You really don't want to loan it to him, but you say, "Yes." anyway.

\_\_\_\_\_ 8. You get angry with your boss, so you stay especially busy when he is around so you don't have to look at or talk to him.

\_\_\_\_\_ 9. One of your fellow employees asks you to go to lunch with him. You don't really like to be around the person, but you go anyway.

\_\_\_\_\_ 10. When your boss comes down on you, you turn around and take things out on others.

# Personal Boundaries

Now it's time for us to help you define healthy boundaries that will help you deal with issues that have plagued you for some time. Follow the directives below to begin the process of boundary clarification and development. Be ready to share at least one of your boundary issues with the group. Remember that it is essential to have a consequence if someone tries to breach your boundary.

**Individual Activity: Boundary Needs**

Using information from the previous worksheets and your own areas of concern list the ten specific areas for which you want to set a boundary.

1.

2.

3.

4.

5.

6.

7.

8.

9.

10.

# My Boundaries Worksheet

**Instructions**

1. Place the issue or boundary need in the left-hand column.
2. Identify the boundary you want to set in the right-hand column.
3. Make sure to include a consequence if someone tests your boundary.

## Personal Boundaries

| Boundary Need | Boundary |
|---|---|
|  |  |
|  |  |
|  |  |
|  |  |
|  |  |
|  |  |
|  |  |
|  |  |
|  |  |

A copy of this form is in the appendices.

# Boundary Weaknesses and Your Personal Code

Instructions

1. Read each of the Codependency or Coping types listed below.
2. After you have considered them, determine which one you exhibit most of the time in most situations.
3. Put a check next to the one most like you. If none of them are like you that's good.
4. If there is more than one you can check those also.

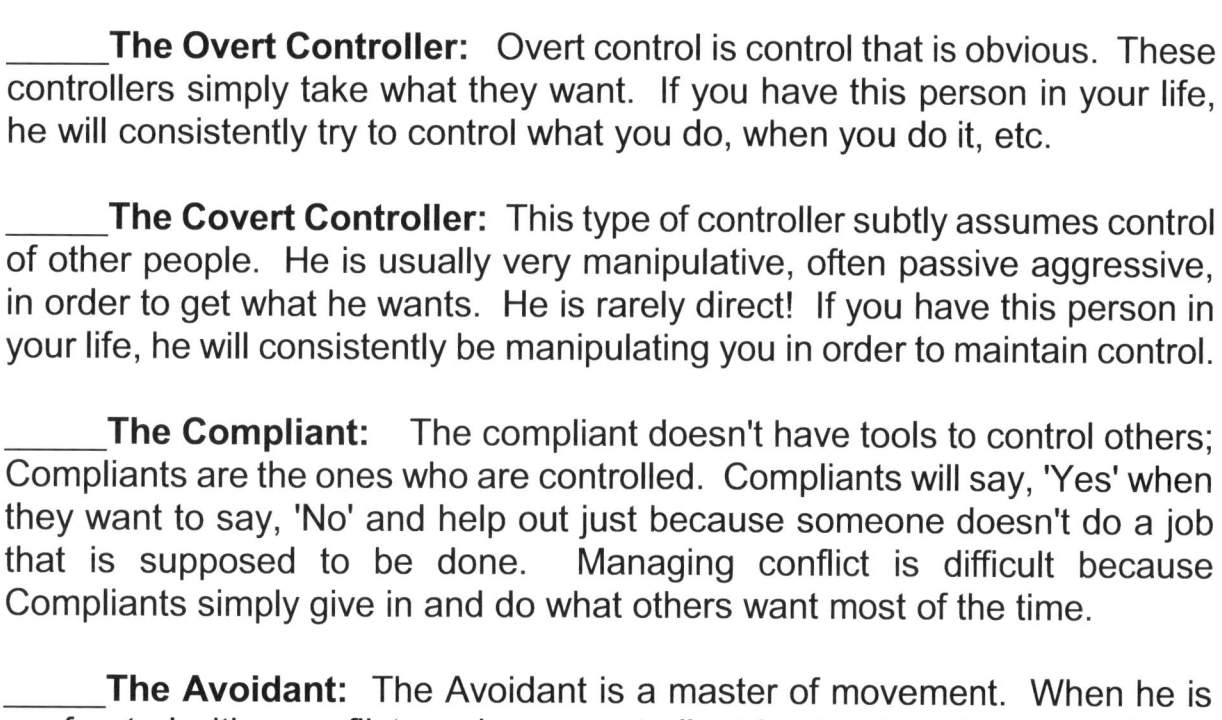

\_\_\_\_\_**The Overt Controller:** Overt control is control that is obvious. These controllers simply take what they want. If you have this person in your life, he will consistently try to control what you do, when you do it, etc.

\_\_\_\_\_**The Covert Controller:** This type of controller subtly assumes control of other people. He is usually very manipulative, often passive aggressive, in order to get what he wants. He is rarely direct! If you have this person in your life, he will consistently be manipulating you in order to maintain control.

\_\_\_\_\_**The Compliant:** The compliant doesn't have tools to control others; Compliants are the ones who are controlled. Compliants will say, 'Yes' when they want to say, 'No' and help out just because someone doesn't do a job that is supposed to be done. Managing conflict is difficult because Compliants simply give in and do what others want most of the time.

\_\_\_\_\_**The Avoidant:** The Avoidant is a master of movement. When he is confronted with a conflict or when a controller tries to take advantage of him, he simply disappears. He may leave, go to another room, go golfing, or find a way to be too busy to deal with the situation. Regardless, if there is a way out, he will take it. As a result, managing conflict is very difficult.

Use the **Self-Monitoring by Frequency for One Behavior Per Week** on page 119 to catch yourself doing these things on a weekly basis. This will help you reduce how often they will occur.

# Other-Oriented Overt Control and Boundary Damage

Overt control is control that is obvious. Let's look at some overt ways that control can be used against you. Read the following overt methods that controllers can use and put a checkmark next to any overt control methods that others have used to control you in some way.

\_\_\_\_\_**Assumption of Control**--You just assume that you are the best suited for making the decision, doing the job, etc. so you take control.

\_\_\_\_\_**The Computer**--Computer Controllers use reason and logic to hammer their point home. They 'prove their point' and dare anyone to question them.

\_\_\_\_\_**Direct Attack**--Direct Attack Controllers find the other persons weakness and then exploit them. This can take on the form of a verbal, physical or emotional attack.

\_\_\_\_\_**Badgering Controller**--Badgering Controllers simply tell you what they want over and over again until your resistance is completely broken down. They simply wear you out.

\_\_\_\_\_**Intimidating Controller**--The Intimidating Controller often uses physical assault or threat of assault to get you to do what they want. After all, they are 'bigger and/or meaner' and could very easily hurt you, so you better do what they want--or else!

\_\_\_\_\_**Perfectionistic Controller**--The Perfectionistic Controller will set standards for others that are difficult if not impossible to attain and then discredit the individual when he can't attain to the set standards.

\_\_\_\_\_**Control by Guilt**--Control by Guilt occurs when you put a person on the spot knowing that their guilt will 'compel' them to do what you want. You play on that guilt to make sure that the person does what you want.

Note: A compliant often accommodates, people pleases, or does what others want.

# Example of How to Address an Overt Controller

| Addressing the Overt Controller ||
|---|---|
| Overt Control Type: | Badgering Controller |
| Write down an example of a Situation where this has been used against you. | My wife keeps asking for a new piece of jewelry over and over and won't stop until I get something for her. |
| Write down what your response is in that situation and what usually happens. | My response is usually 'No, we can't afford it right now.' However, she asks me over and over and I usually give in even if I can't afford it. |
| Identify an assertive technique that you could use to counter that covert control type if it occurs again in the future. | Standing firm |
| Write down exactly how you would use that technique if this situation occurs again. | Mary "I really would like to get that ring I was looking at. Cold we please get it for me? John After the first request say, "We have already spent way too much money over budget for jewelry. We can put that on the list for your birthday or Christmas. However, I must be more careful with how we are spending our money." Repeat as needed. Stand firm. |

# Other-Oriented Overt Control and Boundary Damage Worksheet

**Instructions**

1. Write down the overt control that either you use against others or that others use against you.
2. Write down how you will attempt to address this form of overt control next time

| Addressing the Overt Controller ||
|---|---|
| Overt Control Type: | |
| Write down an example of a Situation where this has been used against you: | |
| Write down what your response is in that situation and what usually happens. | |
| Identify an assertive technique that you could use to counter that covert control type if it occurs again in the future. | |
| Write down exactly how you would use that technique if this situation occurs again. | |

A copy of this form is in the appendices.

# Other-Oriented Covert Control and Boundary Damage

Covert control is usually very subtle. This type of control can be insidious because the person can 'look' like he is not really controlling, when in fact he is. Read the following covert methods that controllers often use and put a checkmark next to any covert control method that others have used to control you in some way.

_____**Detaching Controller**--As a Detaching Controller you control others by taking yourself away from people who care for you. You may ignore the person, not communicate, withhold something they want or need, refuse to resolve a conflict or any other number of things that make the person miserable. You do this until you get what you want!

_____**Deceitful Controller**--The Deceitful Controller will cheat, steal or lie to get what they want. They will hide information that is damaging to themselves and make up information that is helpful. Anything that will help them get what they want. These deceptions can range from subtle omissions of the truth to blatant lies.

_____**Manipulative Controller**--The Manipulative Controller controls people by subtly doing things that keep them from doing something that you don't want them to do. For instance, if you don't want your partner to go to a certain meeting you may schedule an 'important appointment, dinner or etc.' that you partner must also attend. You may also accidently lose your partners keys when they need to go somewhere you don't want them to go.

_____**Martyring Guilt**--Martyrs who use guilt covertly seem to be out of control because of their pain and discomfort. However, they use those very things to get you to do whatever they want. They will play on your guilt, by telling you how uncomfortable they are, how much pain they are in, how they are emotionally hurting and anything else that will cause you to finally do what they want.

____**The Negative Hook**--Controllers use the Negative Hook to manipulate you. The funny thing about this manipulation is that it starts out positive and ends up shaming or negative in some way. This type of Controller puts a 'but' at the end of a positive statement. Although the statement outwardly looks positive, in reality it is an extremely damaging negative statement. For instance, 'Honey, you sure look gorgeous in that dress tonight, your weight you've gained doesn't show much in that dress!'

## Example of How to Address the Covert Controller

| Addressing the Covert Controller ||
|---|---|
| Covert Control Type: | Martyring Guilt |
| Write down an example of a Situation where this has been used against you. | My Husband was upset about something at work, so he wanted me to stay home instead of having my girl's night out. He does this a lot. |
| Write down what your response in that situation an what usually happens. | I usually cancel my time with the girls, but when I stay home he does not interact with me much at all. |
| Identify an assertive technique that you could use to counter that covert control type if it occurs again in the future. | The Three Step Technique |
| Write down exactly how you would use that technique if this situation occurs again. | "I really need to spend time with my friends. It makes me feel better and I know I respond better to you when I do." "I get frustrated and lonely for female companionship and I know it makes me a bit irritable when I don't spend time with them." "I know you would rather me stay home, but I really need to be with my friends on girl's night out." |

# Other-Oriented Covert Control and Boundary Damage Worksheet

**Instructions**

1. Write down the covert control that either you use against others or that others use against you.
2. Write down how you will attempt to address this form of covert control next time

| **Addressing the Covert Controller** | |
|---|---|
| Covert Control Type: | |
| Write down an example of a Situation where this has been used against you: | |
| Write down what your response in that situation an what usually happens. | |
| Identify an assertive technique that you could use to counter that covert control type if it occurs again in the future. | |
| Write down exactly how you would use that technique if this situation occurs again. | |

A copy of this form is in the appendices.

# Self-Oriented Overt Control and Boundary Damage

Overt control is control that is obvious. These controllers simply take what they want. Controllers are people who need to take power away from others so that they can have their own way. Read the following overt methods that controllers use and put a check next to any that you use:

_____**Assumption of Control**—Those who use Assumption of Control assume that they are best suited for making a decision, doing the job, etc. so they take control.

_____**The Computer**--Computer Controllers use reason and logic to hammer their point home. They 'prove their point' and dare anyone to question them.

_____**Direct Attack**--Direct Attack Controllers find the other person's weakness and then exploit them. This can take on the form of a verbal, physical or emotional attack.

_____**Badgering Controller**--Badgering Controllers simply tell you what they want over and over again until your resistance is completely broken down. They simply wear you out.

_____**Intimidating Controller**--The Intimidating Controller often uses physical assault or threat of assault to get you to do what they want. After all, they are 'bigger and/or meaner' and could very easily hurt you, so you better do what they want--or else!

_____**Perfectionistic Controller**--The Perfectionistic Controller will set standards for others that are difficult if not impossible to attain and then discredit the individual when he can't attain to the set standards.

_____**Control by Guilt**--Control by Guilt occurs when you put a person on the spot knowing that their guilt will 'compel' them to do what you want. You play on that guilt to make sure that the person does what you want.

# Example of How to Reduce Overt Control

| Reducing Overt Control ||
|---|---|
| Overt Control Type: | Badgering Controller |
| Write down an example of a Situation where you have used this with another person. | I keep asking for a new piece of jewelry over and over and won't stop until I get what I want. |
| Write down what the other person usually says or does in that situation and what usually happens. | My husband tries to say, 'No', but eventually gives in. |
| What can you do to reduce this particular type of overt control in similar situations in the future? | I need to recognize that my husband is trying to stay within budget. I know he just wants to make sure that we don't overspend and make it difficult to pay bills. |
| Write down exactly how you would respond in a reasonable way that does not include any form of control. What words would you use to respond? | When he says, 'No' or 'Not right now' I have to respect that.<br><br>Mary "Ok, but it would be nice if you could make that a birthday present for me. I would really appreciate it. |

# Self-Oriented Overt Control and Boundary Damage Worksheet

**Instructions**

1. Write down the overt control that either you use against others.
2. Write down how you will attempt to reduce this form of overt control next time

| Reducing Overt Control | |
|---|---|
| Overt Control Type: | |
| Write down an example of a Situation where you have used this with another person. | |
| Write down what the other person usually says or does in that situation and what usually happens. | |
| What can you do to reduce this particular type of overt control in similar situations in the future? | |
| Write down exactly how you would respond in a reasonable way that does not include any form of control. What words would you use to respond? | |

A copy of this form is in the appendices.

# Self-Oriented Covert Control and Boundary Damage

Covert control is usually very subtle and is often used in combination with **Overt Control**. This type of control can be insidious because the person can 'look' like he is not really controlling, when in fact he is. Let's look at some covert ways that control can be used. Read the following covert methods that controllers use and put a check next to any that you use.

\_\_\_\_\_**Detaching Controller**--As a Detaching Controller you control others by taking yourself away from people who care for you. You may ignore the person, not communicate, withhold something they want or need, refuse to resolve a conflict or any other number of things that make the person miserable. You do this until you get what you want!

\_\_\_\_\_**Deceitful Controller**--The Deceitful Controller will cheat, steal or lie to get what they want. They will hide information that is damaging to themselves and make up information that is helpful. Anything that will help them get what they want. These deceptions can range from subtle omissions of the truth to blatant lies.

\_\_\_\_\_**Manipulative Controller**--The Manipulative Controller controls people by subtly doing things that keep them from doing something that you don't want them to do. For instance, if you don't want your partner to go to a certain meeting you may schedule an 'important appointment, dinner or etc.' that you partner must also attend. You may also accidently lose your partners keys when they need to go somewhere you don't want them to go.

\_\_\_\_\_**Martyring Guilt**--Martyrs who use guilt covertly seem to be out of control because of their pain and discomfort. However, they use those very things to get you to do whatever they want. They will play on your guilt, by telling you how uncomfortable they are, how much pain they are in, how they are emotionally hurting and anything else that will cause you to finally do what they want.

_____**The Negative Hook**--Controllers use the Negative Hook to manipulate you. The funny thing about this manipulation is that it starts out positive and ends up shaming or negative in some way. This type of Controller puts a 'but' at the end of a positive statement. Although the statement outwardly looks positive, in reality it is an extremely damaging negative statement. For instance, 'Honey, you sure look gorgeous in that dress tonight, your weight you've gained doesn't show much in that dress!'

# Example of How to Reduce Covert Control

| Reducing Covert Control ||
|---|---|
| Overt Control Type: | Detaching Controller |
| Write down an example of a Situation where you have used this with another person. | Every time I know I can't win in a conflict, I find a way to change the topic or I explain that I have something pressing I need to take care of that is work related. I know that if nothing changes, I will get my way. |
| Write down what the other person usually says or does in that situation and what usually happens. | Wife wants to sit down and discuss a problem. I know that it will take time and I just don't want to deal with it. |
| What can you do to reduce this particular type of overt control in similar situations in the future? | I need to recognize that my wife is simply trying to take care of things that need to be done. A decision has to be made. I just need to set time aside to address the issue, even when I don't want to. |
| Write down exactly how you would respond in a reasonable way that does not include any form of control. What words would you use to respond? | When my wife says we need to discuss a specific issue I will say, "OK. Let me think about it first. Right after dinner we can sit down and discuss this. Is that time ok with you?" |

# Self-Oriented Covert Control and Boundary Damage Worksheet

**Instructions**

1. Write down the covert control that either you use against others.
2. Write down how you will attempt to reduce this form of covert control next time

| Reducing Covert Control | |
|---|---|
| Covert Control Type: | |
| Write down an example of a Situation where you have used this with another person. | |
| Write down what the other person usually says or does in that situation and what usually happens. | |
| What can you do to reduce this particular type of overt control in similar situations in the future? | |
| Write down exactly how you would respond in a reasonable way that does not include any form of control. What words would you use to respond? | |

A copy of this form is in the appendices.

# Reducing Control Issues

Your control issues have caused damage for both you and those around you for a long time. If you believe that your controlling ways have damaged any relationships, then complete the following.

Which of the above Overt and Covert control methods do you use most often? List then below!

Take another look at the above self-oriented control issues write down how each of the controlling methods you use have caused damage with a personal relationship, friends and/or work.

Write a short letter to someone you have a relationship with (romantic, friendship, work, etc.). Share how you have been controlling in their life and how you want to change it for the betterment of that relationship.

You can, 1) Send or read it to the person or, 2) You can throw it away after writing it. If you want to reduce your control you obviously need to share your letter.

**Question after Sharing**

What is something I can do that will make me less controlling when I am around you?   Write down their response.




Once you know what the person wants, do your best for a week to see how well it works.  I it works you may want to continue.  You may also want to write a letter to other people you have hurt and ask the same question.

# Common Yet Effective Boundary Statements

To make sure your boundaries are working for you, it is important that you have the tools necessary to stand up for them. Sometimes you simply need to communicate exactly what you want or don't want to maintain a boundary (gentle approach). Other times you may need to set firm consequences (firm approach). Here are some examples of how you can verbally protect your boundaries.

### Gentle Approach

- "Thanks for asking, but I'd rather not talk about (or do) that."
- "I'd rather not do that, but I appreciate you wanting me to be part of it."
- "I would appreciate it if we could talk about something else."

### Firm Approach

If the person doesn't listen to you and still tries to breech your boundary you must get firm and provide a consequence.

- "No! If you ask again, I will have to leave."
- "I'm not interested in doing that. If you ask again, I will have to leave."
- "I'm not comfortable with that. If you ask me again, I will have to ask you to leave."
- "I'm not going to talk about that. If you want to spend time with me, you must respect that this topic is off limits at this time. If you persist, I will not want to spend time with you again."
- "I'm not willing to do that. I don't want to spend time with people who try to make me do things that are uncomfortable to me."
- "Please don't ask me about that again. I told you last time you asked that I'd rather not talk about it. If you persist, we will not be able to spend as much time together as we have in the past."
- "It's not that I'm not interested in spending time with you, it's just that I have other plans. Ask again in a week or so. IF you can't do what I'm asking, just don't call at all."

# Boundary Consequences and Considerations

There are multiple consequences that you can consider if you are wanting to develop and maintain your boundaries. Here are a few things that you may want to think about as you go about the task of developing boundaries.

1. When you finally begin to establish healthy boundaries, controllers and people who can't handle change will resist the change in you.

2. When you start to get angry, look to see if someone is trying to violate one of your boundaries.

3. Allow yourself to be drawn to those who respect your boundaries. You'll quickly realize that with healthy people you won't have to defend your boundaries so much.

4. You will begin to feel safe around people who have healthy boundaries and values. It will also be refreshing.

> *Remember, boundaries without consequences are not effective.*

# When Boundaries Don't Work

There are times that your boundaries are simply not working. What's causing the problem? Is it something you are doing or is the person just not respecting your boundaries? Consider the following possibilities. If you are doing any of these, it could cause your boundary setting to be ineffective. Check any that you believe you do!

___You have no consequence for violating your boundary.

___You have a consequence, but you fail to give it.

___You don't follow through with your consequences on a consistent basis.

___You feel bad for, or threatened by, the person and fail to give the consequence.
___You threaten consequences that are to unrealistic to carry out.

___You set a consequence and then change your mind.

___You reinforce negative behavior that bothers you by laughing, putting up with or by taking no action when behaviors bother you.
___You violate your own boundaries by participating in activities that are contradictory to your personal values, beliefs, etc.
___Your tone you use when setting boundaries is not firm or you are critical or negative in some way.
___Your body language encourages the person to dismiss your boundary.

___Using your consequences to change your behavior instead of altering other people's behavior.
___People around you do not support your boundaries.

**When Boundaries Don't Work:** Look at the statements you checked on the previous page. Pick the top three (but do all when you can) and list them below. Below write down what you will do to address each of those issues for your own good.

| Fixing Boundary Issues Worksheet ||
|---|---|
| Boundary Issue Identified | How I will fix it! |
|  |  |
|  |  |
|  |  |
|  |  |
|  |  |
|  |  |
|  |  |

A copy of this form is in the appendices.

# CONFLICT MANAGEMENT

## Section Four

This last section of the workbook describes what conflict management is all about and how you can more effectively use it when you have conflict that cannot be resolved using assertive skills alone. There are numerous conflict management techniques that can be of tremendous benefit to you when you are experiencing problems. The topics covered in this section are as follows:

- Preventing Conflict — 127
- Steps for Addressing Conflict — 128
- Rules for Conflict — 129
- Reduce Conflict Triggers — 130
- Self-Monitoring by Frequency for One Behavior Per Week — 132
- Learn to Listen — 134
- Active Listening Skills — 135
- Non-Verbal Listening Skills — 136
- Keep Yourself Under Control — 137
- Strategies for Inner Peace — 138
    - Your Vacation Paradise — 139
    - The Chair: Breathing and Relaxing for Healing — 141
    - The Quick Relaxation Technique — 142
- Feelings and Conflict Resolution — 143
- Non-Productive Conflict Styles — 144
- Addressing Non-Productive Conflict Styles — 145
- Time Outs for Conflict — 147

- ➢ Resolution, Compromise or Management — 151
  - Conflict Resolution Methods — 152
  - The Learning Conversation — 153
  - The Communication Game — 154
  - The Five Step Conflict Resolution Technique Described — 157
  - The Five Step Conflict Resolution Technique Worksheet — 158
  - Conflict Resolution and Decision-Making Worksheet — 160
  - Problem Solving and the Two Column Technique — 161
  - Problem Solving and the Two Column Technique Worksheet — 162
  - Compromise Methods — 163
  - The Will to Compromise — 164
  - Compromise Model for Conflict Management — 166
  - Compromise Model for Conflict Management Worksheet — 168
- ➢ Conflict Management Methods — 170
- ➢ Conflict Management Method Options — 171
- ➢ Keeping Track of Decisions — 172
- ➢ Conflicts with Personal Decision Making — 174
  - Seven Step Problem Solving Method — 175
  - T-Chart for Decision Making — 176

# Preventing Conflict

It is neither possible nor desirable to prevent all forms of conflict in your life. In addition to being assertive (which has already been discussed), there are other methods for preventing or minimizing the amount of conflict in your life. There are five basic things that you can do that will help you avoid unnecessary conflict. They are:

- Initially, be kind and gentle with your words. It may reduce how much others react to you in a negative way.
- Listen, ask questions. Seek to understand the other person's point of view.
- Learn Assertive skills that protect you from conflict.

- Minimize contact with people who are critical, aggressive, undependable, not trustworthy, etc.
- Set boundaries and consequences in advance for situations that you know you will face often.

**Individual Exercise**

State one thing that you could do that would help you improve in each area listed above.

1.

2.

3.

4.

5.

# Steps for Addressing Conflict

There are certain steps that you can use for good conflict resolution. If you simply follow these directives you will find that your conflict will be more easily dealt with on a day to day basis.

**Steps**

When you begin to experience a conflict, you must take immediate action if you are to overcome the problem. There are certain steps of action that you must follow if you want to have a chance of success.

1. Stop the conflict so that it won't get worse.
2. Get out of your anger or critical mode. No name calling, no belittling, no aggressiveness, etc. You will never be able to handle conflict well when you are angry or if you are triggering the other person to be upset. The less angry you are, the easier it will be to effectively deal with the problem.
3. Sit down and address your concern kindly and calmly and simply say what you believe needs to happen to resolve it. 'Please' and 'It would be nice if…' are both good starting points.
4. If both of you feel strongly about what needs to happen, talk. Ask the question, "What is it about this particular issue that makes it so important to you?" LISTEN, don't think about your counter. Ask questions to clarify what the other person is saying. Don't worry about resolving it at the moment. Learn why it is important to each of you and the reasons that cause it to be so important. There will be times that one person's reasons why it is so important is so compelling that the other person will willingly give in. Even if that doesn't happen, you will have a better understanding of what causes that person to feel so strongly about this issue.
5. If after your discussion you are still stuck and can't decide how to deal with the issue you need to utilize, 1) a Conflict Resolution Method, 2) a Compromise Method, or 3) a Management Method that will lead you to a final solution.

# Rules for Conflict

When you have a conflict and you use healthy, acceptable rules to aid you in resolving the problem you will have a much better chance for successful resolution. You will be effectively using conflict resolution skills. Here are some ground rules that set up a healthy situation for a discussion so that a conflict can be resolved.

1. Agree to resolve the conflict!
2. Take turns talking! DON'T INTERRUPT!!! Don't talk over each other!!!!!
3. Discuss only one topic at a time. Make sure it is resolved before you discuss any other topic. Set a time limit of fifteen to thirty minutes maximum. Take a break and come back to it at a designated time.
4. Don't try to win. If one partner wins the couple loses.
5. Define the topic to be discussed. Both should agree on the definition.
6. Keep to the here and now (don't bring up the past).
7. Focus on the problem, not the other person (do not attack the other person's character)--no name calling!
8. Call foul when your partner breaks a rule or attacks you.
9. Do not counter attack if the other person attacks you (stay in your adult rational mode).
11. If you find yourself tensing up take a time out and relax a little. Don't let yourself get bent out of shape to the point that you can't discuss things rationally.
12. Be clear and truthful about what is bothering you and what you really need.
13. Do not leave mentally or physically until both parties feel like the problem has been resolved or has been tabled.
14. When the immediate conflict is resolved don't continue to discuss it. Let it go!!!!!
15. Write down the solution you have both agreed to in a spiral notebook entitled, Conflict Solutions. Write down the conflict, the resolution, date it and both of you sign it. If the same issue come up again refer to your Conflict Solutions notebook. Don't spend hours finding a solution you have already solved.

# Reduce Conflict Triggers

There are several conflict triggers that we all use unintentionally and sometimes intentionally. When used, these triggers promote conflict. Read the following and check any of them that you feel you do in any relationship that you have.

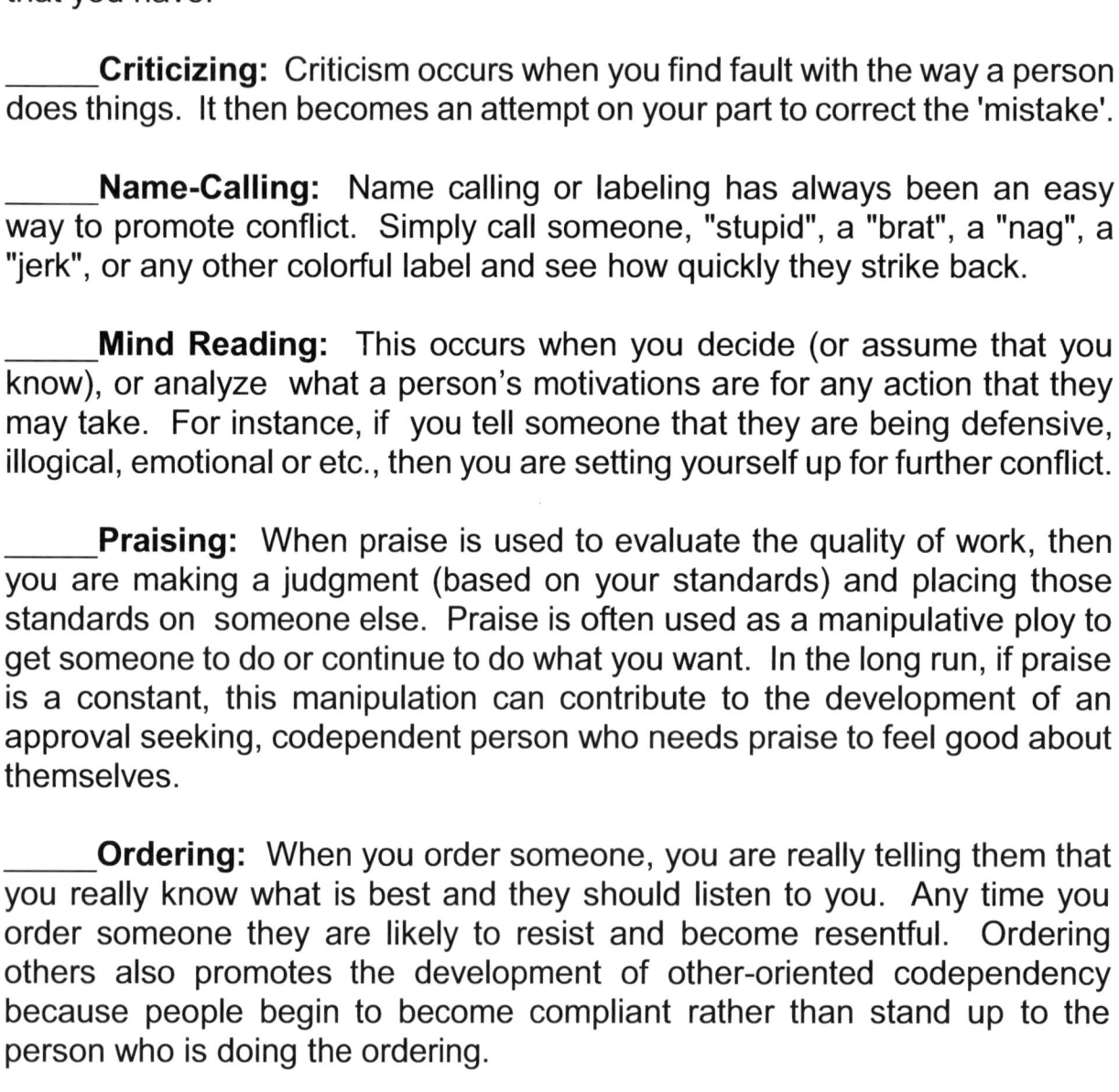

_____**Criticizing:** Criticism occurs when you find fault with the way a person does things. It then becomes an attempt on your part to correct the 'mistake'.

_____**Name-Calling:** Name calling or labeling has always been an easy way to promote conflict. Simply call someone, "stupid", a "brat", a "nag", a "jerk", or any other colorful label and see how quickly they strike back.

_____**Mind Reading:** This occurs when you decide (or assume that you know), or analyze what a person's motivations are for any action that they may take. For instance, if you tell someone that they are being defensive, illogical, emotional or etc., then you are setting yourself up for further conflict.

_____**Praising:** When praise is used to evaluate the quality of work, then you are making a judgment (based on your standards) and placing those standards on someone else. Praise is often used as a manipulative ploy to get someone to do or continue to do what you want. In the long run, if praise is a constant, this manipulation can contribute to the development of an approval seeking, codependent person who needs praise to feel good about themselves.

_____**Ordering:** When you order someone, you are really telling them that you really know what is best and they should listen to you. Any time you order someone they are likely to resist and become resentful. Ordering others also promotes the development of other-oriented codependency because people begin to become compliant rather than stand up to the person who is doing the ordering.

_____**Threatening**:  When a person is threatened, they understand that if they don't do what you want there will be some consequence.  In the long run, threatening also produces compliant, other oriented people who don't want to rock the boat.  They will do anything to avoid confrontation.

_____**Moralizing**:  When you are threatened by someone who moralizes you begin to sense that they are setting standards for you and then letting you know if you don't live up to those standards.  "Shoulds" and "oughts" are often part of the communication either explicitly or implicitly. Moralizing often produces a guilty feeling for those on the receiving end.

_____**Advising**:  When you send advice to another human being you are sending a subtle message that they aren't intelligent enough, educated enough, etc. to handle the situation.  Advising should only occur when the person actually asks for it.  Even when that occurs it's smart to ask again to make sure that the person really wants your input.

_____**Diverting**:  Whenever we are uncomfortable with the content of a communication, it is easy for us to change the topic.  Changing the topic is a diversion or an avoidance of the uncomfortable.  People develop numerous methods for diversion.   This is avoidance!  Some examples are:

- Simply exiting the conversation!
- "That reminds me of......"
- "Speaking of....."
- "I remember a time when....."

_____**Logical Argument**:  When a person is emotionally upset it is often the wrong time to try to communicate 'the logical solution'.  However, those who thrive on logic see this as the method of choice and the end result is a breakdown of communication and a lost chance to begin healing and resolve a conflict. This only make people more upset rather than settling them down.

Use the **Self-Monitoring by Frequency for One Behavior Per Week** on the next page to help you keep track of how often you exhibit any of these conflict triggers.   Simply knowing that these trigger conflict and by keeping track of them can help you reduce how often you exhibit them on a daily basis.

# Self-Monitoring by Frequency for One Behavior Per Week

**Name:**                                                          **Beginning Date:**

## Instructions

1. Prepare yourself and start on a Sunday so that you can more easily keep track for specific weeks at a time.
2. Write down the behavior or words you are wanting to reduce the frequency of in the space provided.
3. Mark across the number each time you exhibit the behavior you are trying to reduce.
4. You probably won't exhibit one of the chosen behaviors ten times in a day. It is possible, but not probable. If it did happen simply put a Plus sign + next to the 10 to show that you exhibited that behavior more than ten times.
5. The goal is to reduce the times you exhibit the behavior or use the words that has caused you or other's problems.

| Behavior/Words to be Measured | |
|---|---|
| **Day** | **Times Exhibited Today** |
| Sunday | 1  2  3  4  5  6  7  8  9  10 |
| Monday | 1  2  3  4  5  6  7  8  9  10 |
| Tuesday | 1  2  3  4  5  6  7  8  9  10 |
| Wednesday | 1  2  3  4  5  6  7  8  9  10 |
| Thursday | 1  2  3  4  5  6  7  8  9  10 |
| Friday | 1  2  3  4  5  6  7  8  9  10 |
| Saturday | 1  2  3  4  5  6  7  8  9  10 |

*This form can be used for any words or behaviors you are wanting to reduce or discontinue. A copy in in the appendices.*

**Helpful Option:** You can also identify a positive opposite that you can say when you catch yourself using the conflict trigger you are attempting to discontinue. Say it ten times each time you catch yourself.

Instructions;

1. Place the identified conflict trigger in the left-hand column.
2. Identify a Positive opposite for each trigger.
3. Each time you catch yourself using the conflict trigger
    - Accept you said or did it and let it go.
    - Say your positive opposite ten times to yourself

| Conflict Trigger | Positive Opposite |
|---|---|
|  |  |
|  |  |
|  |  |
|  |  |
|  |  |

You can use the above chart for any conflict trigger you identify.
It can also be used for any unwanted behavior
that you want to reduce.

# Learn to Listen

There are two basic areas of listening that you can develop if you want to reduce conflict and produce greater communication with others. They are:

- Even when the person is angry, very upset, etc. it is important for you to focus on what is being said. Don't argue, learn. What is the person upset about? Ask questions. Explore their story. Learn without judging. Be the one who listens intently and shows that you want to know why that person has that stance. Use the phrase 'Do you mean?' often in order to clarify what is being said. Listen for feelings. Ask if your perception is right. When they are finished, summarize what you learned and listen if the person says you didn't get it. Say, 'Explain to me the part I missed please.' Listen again. Don't be in a hurry to share your side.
- Use active listening skills. Listen, don't think, just listen to the content and for the underlying emotions.
- Watch for non-verbal signs that sometimes communicate more than words. Don't assume though. Never assume!!!!

**Individual Exercise**

Before we go on determine one thing you could do that would improve each area listed above.

# Active Listening Skills

Good listening is evident when you have received what another person has sent. Listening occurs when you are concentrating, accepting, able to repeat and as possible identify the underlying emotions regarding what the other person has said. There are four parts to active listening. They are:

**Concentration:** Focus on what the person is saying. You can't be thinking about your response. Listen to the words and what they mean. Try to figure out what the person is attempting to communicate.

**Accepting:** Accept what the person is saying. It is their perception, and it is important to that person. A simple nod of the head suggesting that you agree or understand what the person is saying is important. However, that doesn't mean that you AGREE. It means that you can accept that what the person says is Truth to him, but it may not be truth to you.

**Repeating:** Repeating what you have heard is not as easy as many think. It actually takes good listening skills and effort to get it right. Try to repeat back what the person says using their words, not yours. Keep it as close to their communication as you can. For instance,

"I hear you saying, (fill in the blank with their words). Is that right?" If you get it right the person is usually happy, thankful, less angry, etc. If you are wrong the person may get upset, restate what was said or give up. So, it is important to get it right as often as possible. Listen carefully and be able to say back what you have heard.

**Underlying Emotions:** The last thing you may want to attempt is to identify the underlying feelings behind the words. If you can identify the specific feeling, you may be able to better understand the purpose of the words. For instance, you may hear, "I can't believe that you don't do more things to help around the house." The content is obvious. However, what is the underlying feeling? Is it anger, frustration, anxiety? She may be angry at you for not helping. She may simply need more help and isn't sure how to get it. You may need to explore her feelings to determine the underlying need behind her words and feelings.

# Non-Verbal Listening Skills

Gabor listed six 'softeners' or non-verbal gestures that communicate that you are interested in what another person is saying. They are as follows:

**Gestures**             **Meaning**

___ S =                  Smile

___ O =                  Open Posture

___ F =                  Forward Lean

___ T =                  Touch

___ E =                  Eye Contact

___ N =                  Nod

**Individual Exercise**

Look at the gestures above and then put a check next to each of them that you feel you do not do well when you are communicating with someone else. Pick one that you are willing to diligently work on until you have internalized it. When you are successful, pick another one and work on it. Practice in a mirror, in the Inner Sanctum (Going to the Movies), and in real life.

# Keep Yourself Under Control

True peace and serenity comes from within. If you don't have a healthy love for yourself and others you won't find inner peace. When you look within do you see peace, contentment or do you see turmoil and pain. Inner peace comes from an acceptance of who you are and where you are in your life. That doesn't mean that you can't improve or want for more. It is obvious that we need to develop the process of unconditional love in our lives so there is room for change. The acceptance that is being suggested simply means that you should be content with where you are and as doors to new horizons open take advantage of the new possibilities and continue to grow. Inner peace also comes from when we learn to shut the brain noise off. Many of us find it nearly impossible to, 'BE STILL' and sense a quietness within. Accomplishing that task will pay dividends throughout your life. If we are to learn how to be still so that we can have opportunity to enjoy inner peace, you must practice on a daily basis.

List three ways you could or have practiced inner peace.

1.

2.

3.

# Strategies for Inner Peace and Change

Being calm, peaceful, and still are all important if you are to be able to handle life's problems in a way that will help you be more prepared for the daily pitfalls that you will face. The more stressed out you are, the more apt you are to react to conflict instead of being calm and reasoning out what needs to be done to address the issue. Here are three methods that, when practiced, can help you stay peaceful and calm when you are faced with conflict.

- Visualizing Your Vacation Paradise
- The Chair: Breathing and Relaxing for Healing
- The Quick Relaxation Technique

**My Plan**

What will you do on a consistent basis to keep your overall stress level down? Be honest with yourself. Read more about the three techniques listed above before you decide. If you have a technique that works for you and want to use it, then choose it to be your primary technique. Only write it down if you are willing to do something.

# Your Vacation Paradise

This visualization is meant to be used to enhance your relaxation. This was initially developed as part of the Inner Sanctum. However, you can use this technique without using the Inner Sanctum. Simply Identify a place that you have been to, or would like to go to that is extremely relaxing and peaceful. Once you have a place in mind follow the instructions below.

**Building Your Vacation Paradise**

First, you must identify what your vacation paradise looks like. There are many options. Some examples to consider for your Vacation Paradise might are:

- Beach Scene
- Cabin facing a beautiful meadow
- In the forest
- Looking at a beautiful lake
- Looking at a mountain
- Laying in your backyard swaying in hammock
- Looking out over a beautiful lake

NOTE: You can have multiple relaxation locations if you desire. Just put buttons on the side of your Vacation Paradise door for each location.

Once you pick your vacation paradise spot there are some key points that you should consider.

1. Remember, you should start with the picture image and see yourself in your personal paradise. Try to see color. Make it as real as it can be.
2. Once you get the picture in your mind it is time for you to 'step into it'. Instead of seeing the picture, you experience the scene as if you were sitting or lying there. It becomes first person. Don't worry about all your senses yet…that comes next. Get the image down first person before you try to include senses.
3. Last, you need to bring your senses into the scene. Work on each sense until it becomes as real as if you were actually there. Add

motion (not too much—trees swaying, birds flying, animals walking, clouds floating by, etc.), smell (if it is the ocean smell the ocean breeze, if mountains smell the earthiness of the mountains, etc.), touch or feel what is around you with your hand and body, hear, e.g., the surf, birds, animals, wind, and taste if it is part of your scene.
4. Work this until you can sense that you are there. All your senses are working. It should seem like you are there. As far as your mind is concerned, if you are doing all those things, you really are there. As a result, your body reacts as if you really are at the beach, the lake, etc. It relaxes just as it would if you were on a real vacation,

Adapted from the **Foundations Workbook – Revised** by F. Russell Crites, Jr.

# The Chair: Breathing and Relaxing for Healing

This strategy was initially developed to use in your inner sanctum. However, you do have a choice. It can be used with or without the Inner Sanctum being part of the strategy. If you want to use it with the Inner Sanctum you must first go to your Inner Sanctum, walk over to the chair, sit in it and from that point you do your relaxation strategy. If you do not use the Inner Sanctum follow the directions below,

1. Close your eyes and begin to totally relax your body. Use your deep breathing exercise if you like.
2. Imagine a large comfortable chair that appears in the room where you were when you closed your eyes. Get a good picture of the chair. It is a large stuffed chair that looks like it will fold up around you when you sit down. It looks very comfortable. It has all kinds of gadgets on it that will help you in the future if you have need of something special. Be creative as to how it can help you.
3. You walk over to the chair, turn around and sit in it. As soon as you do it seems as if the chair is soaking up any tension you have. Feel your body relax as the chair gently squeezes your body starting with your neck, going down to your shoulders and upper back. Enjoy the feeling that you are experiencing. With each second, the chair squeezes and soaks tension your body and mind relaxes more. You allow the chair to massage your whole body…..it continues to soak up the stress.
4. Once the chair has finished its full body massage, focus on your breathing. It is slower. You are more peaceful. Continue to breath slowly as you focus on the total relaxation you feel in your body and mind.
5. Last, simply listen to your breathing as you let your body go and be at complete peace. Stay in this state as long as you like.
6. When you are ready to come back to reality, you may do so by slowly acknowledging your surroundings while your eyes are still closed. When you are ready open your eyes, you will feel much more rested, peaceful and calm than you did before you started.

Adapted from the Foundations Workbook – Revised by F. Russell Crites, Jr.

# Quick Relaxation Technique

This is an easy relaxation strategy that is a favorite among many. You can do it quickly and it can produce good results. However, just like with all such exercises, the longer you use it the more effective it becomes. Here are the basic steps to this technique:

1. Close your eyes and relax as best you can…..take a deep breath and let it out.
2. Now, do a body scan…..from the top of your head to the tips of your toes, one part at a time.
3. First, check your face for any signs of tension……if it is there let it go…take your time and make sure you are good before you continue.
4. Now scan your neck and shoulders………is there any tension there…..let it go….relax.
5. Now check your arms and hands……are they tensed up at all……if so let go…..relax……let the tension melt away.
6. Now check your chest, back and stomach……if you sense any tension relax……let it go.
7. Next, check your thighs and buttocks……if you are holding any tension there let it go.
8. Now check your calf muscles and feet……are they tensed up at all…..if so, relax them…..let the tension go.
9. Now look back over your body. Slowly scan it again from the top of your head to the tips of your toes. If you find any area that is still tense let it go….relax….take your time and let any tension you have melt away.
10. Rescan resistant body parts until you get a level of relaxation that you are satisfied with.
11. Now that you are relaxed take few moments so that your body and mind can enjoy the relaxed sensation.
12. Play out the skill set you want to improve on the Going to the Movies technique. Replay this 5 to 10 times. At a later time, return and do this video clip over and over until it gets very comfortable.
13. When you are ready, open your eyes feeling much more calm and relaxed.

**Adapted from <u>Bipolar or ADHD: Educational and Home Based Strategies for Bipolar Disorder, ADHD and Other Co-Existing Conditions.</u>** By F. Russell Crites, Jr.

# Feelings and Conflict Resolution

It is essential that you deal with a person's feelings first when a conflict is evident. Logic never seems to work when a person is upset. When you do talk keep your message short and to the point. It will be 'digested' easier when there are fewer words to deal with. There are some basic steps that should be followed when you are beginning to deal with a conflict and the person you're opposite of is emotional.

**Step One: Focused Listening**

First, you must be ready to listen. This means that you will listen intently as long as the other person need to talk about their feelings. Remember, conflict resolution does not occur when someone is in an emotional state so take your time and let them talk out their feelings. As you are listening show that you are interested by focusing on what they are saying. Look them in the eye (as long as they are comfortable with it), express your empathy with facial expressions and nod of the head, lean forward and give short responses showing that you are listening.

**Step Two: Conflict Resolution Method Used**

Once the person has 'talked themselves out' of their feeling state then you can begin to use any number of conflict resolution methods that will help you resolve the issue. However, if at any point either person starts to have feelings emerge that are hindering logical resolution then they must be dealt with before you go on. Don't be surprised if you need to go back and deal with feelings several times when you are trying to resolve any conflict. Simply accept it and go on. Remember, feelings are what makes life so special and it is through resolution that our feelings for others are enhanced.

# Non-Productive Conflict Styles

Put a check mark next to the non-productive conflict style that you feel you use the most when you are having personal conflicts.

## NON-PRODUCTIVE STYLES

\_\_\_\_\_**Withdrawal Style:** Anytime either person leaves, in body or mind, so that they don't have to deal with conflict he/she is using the Withdrawal Style.

\_\_\_\_\_**Yielding Style:** The statement, "Whatever you want is okay with me." is a red flag that states that this person has given up. A person who uses this style is usually just tired of losing and resentment is probably growing with each conflict. If a person continues with this style it may lead to serious codependency issues. Usually people develop Other-Oriented codependency when this occurs.

\_\_\_\_\_**Fighting Style:** This occurs when one partner concentrates on attacking the other person. This attack can be either overt or covert. However, he will make the other person look and feel bad until he gets his way. This style also promotes the continuation of self-oriented controlling codependency. It produces serious codependency issues for the one on the receiving end. They usually develop serious Avoidant or Other-Oriented Codependencies.

\_\_\_\_\_**Winning Style:** This is often the other side of the Yielding Style. Winning an argument is more important than being right. Self-Oriented Codependents usually use this form of conflict resolution. Winning keeps the person in charge and in control. This often produces either Avoidant or Other-Oriented codependency in others.

# Addressing Non-Productive Conflict Styles

**Relationships:** Which style does a person you often deal with in life exhibit? List the person and the non-productive style that is used!

| Relationship | Person's Name | Non-Productive Style Used |
|---|---|---|
| Family Member | | |
| A Significant Someone | | |
| A Close Friend | | |
| Someone at Work | | |
| Other: | | |

Instructions

1. Identify the person and the non-productive style used
2. Identify the assertive method you may want to use to minimize the other person's usage of that non-productive style with you!
3. Pick a preferred Conflict method you would want to use in such situations. Keep in mind that you won't always be able to use the one you want, you may have to adjust.

| Person | Non-Productive Style Used | Assertive Method to Use to Address it. | Preferred Conflict Method to use instead. |
|---|---|---|---|
| | | | |
| | | | |
| | | | |
| | | | |

**Relationships:** Which style do you often use with others? List a specific person and the non-productive style that you use with that person!

| Relationship | Person's Name | Non-Productive Style Used |
|---|---|---|
| Family Member | | |
| Significant Someone | | |
| A Close Friend | | |
| Someone at Work | | |
| Other: | | |

A copy of this is in the appendices.

## Reduce the Times You Use a Specific Non-Productive Conflict Style

Go to the appendices and make a copy of the Self-Monitoring by Frequency for One Behavior Per Week and use the monitoring form to catch yourself using the non-productive conflict style. Take your time and gradually get rid of any non-productive conflict style. As you do you will have to work hard to use the Conflict Resolution strategy, Compromise strategy or the Conflict Management strategy.

# Time Outs for Conflict

## Handout

Have you ever tried to resolve or manage conflict when one or both parties are emotionally upset? If you have, you know that it doesn't work. When feelings get in the way solutions for conflict are next to impossible to identify. That's why it is important to take time outs when either person seems to be getting upset. If you don't, it will probably only get worse. So, here are some pointers that may help you with developing a time out that will help both of you when you are trying to come to an agreement regarding a conflict.

## Why Time Outs Don't Always Work

In theory taking a time out can be a very helpful and productive way to improve your chances of resolving a conflict. However, unless both parties take a "proper" time out, it's not going to be helpful. There are a few reasons why "time outs" may not work when you are trying to resolve a conflict:

- The time away is spent ruminating on negative emotions rather than focusing on the core issue
- One or both parties may take a "time out" simply to escape the issue.
- One or both parties may be looking for a way to distract themselves from the pressing problem at hand and use it as a way to move on without addressing the issue.

If either individual spent the time apart focusing on any one of the above three items, once they resume their previous discussion, they would most assuredly end up right back where they were before they parted for the time out because their outlook or perspective hasn't really changed. In fact, an individual may feel even more fueled up and ready to argue rather than seek resolution.

## Things to Avoid

- Following the person who requested a time-out. This inevitably leads to an escalation of conflict. Respect each other's need to get away, but always establish a time to come back so that you can continue your conversation.
- Storming away. If you leave showing how upset you are without explaining why you are leaving, where you are going and if you are coming back or not you simply magnify the problem
- Time-outs done when either of you are not ready. If either of you are over-tired, or under excessive stress it may be best to wait.
- Avoid communicating in an angry tone of voice as you leave for your time out. For instance, "You make me so mad," or "I can't talk to you."

## Agree that Times-Outs are Good and Should Be Used

It is important that the couple establish a mutual understanding that time-outs are not just okay, but important and helpful. Make sure that there is an agreement regarding the use of the time out before you find yourselves in an escalating argument. For example, you could both agree on:

1. When a Time-Out should be used
2. The positive reasons for a time out, which is to change your state of mind, to create space and time to self-soothe and reflect on what to do next, and not to avoid or control the argument,
3. How a time-out could be carried out.

## Understanding the Need and Timing of a Time-Out

The best time for a couple to take a time-out is when there is a shift in the internal state of one or both parties that will put them at the risk of escalating the conversation into an unnecessary or damaging argument. When the conversation is at this critical point, both individuals are at a higher risk of saying something they would regret. This is one of the most important reasons why a time-out should be used.

## The Purpose of a Time Out

A time-out is never a permanent solution for how to resolve or manage conflict in in any relationship. Time-out should be considered a temporary measure that the couple uses to return to a healthier, more positive, constructive frame of mind so that they can address issues.

## What You Should Be doing During a Time-Out

Simply being apart is not the most constructive thing that occurs. It does give you some time to calm down and think, but simply being apart will not lead to resolution or compromise. It takes more than that. There are several things each person should be considering while they are in their time out. For instance:

1. Take time to de-stress. Walk, read a book, work out or do anything that helps you calm down.
2. Think about why you are angry or upset. What is really your underlying motivation for getting so upset? Could it be hurt, fear, sadness? Think about your underlying feelings and how you could share them in a more positive way with your partner
3. Consider how you are responsible for any part of the conflict or problem.
4. Think about the words you are using, your tone of voice, and body language.
5. Are you doing anything that makes it more difficult to rationally discuss the issue?
6. Are your words or actions making it difficult for your partner to listen and accept what you are saying?
7. Is there a solution in the middle that you could suggest that might make it better for both of you instead of being in a win-lose situation?
8. Is there anything you need to change that would make anything regarding this situation better?
9. Do you need to repair any damage before you begin your discussion again? If so, when you return do your best to repair any damage that may have been done.

If you identify anything as you ponder the above, consider how you will communicate it to your partner and how it impacts the current situation. If it causes you to change your stance, explain it to your partner.

## Rules for a Constructive Time-Out

If a time-out is to be effective, it must follow clearly defined procedures that both partners agree to. Not following these rules or procedures can put the relationship at risk.

1. Have a specific way that each of you can call for a time out.
2. Reassure your partner that you are not giving up on the discussion and that you fully intend on returning so that you can continue your discussion.
3. State how long you need to be gone (no less than 30 minutes and no more than 24 hours).
4. Give each other space so that you can review what you should be doing during the time out (See What You Should Be doing During a Time-Out).
5. Return and take time to heal. Apologize if necessary and reaffirm your love and desire to heal.
6. Share what you have learned from your timeout before beginning any kind of resolution or management of the issue.
7. Continue to discuss options to resolve or manage the conflict in a better way for both of you.

Although it is not optimal, sometimes it is better to 'sleep on it' so that you can look at things fresh the next day. Sometimes when you give something time and do some introspection you realize that the issue was not as important as it seemed to be the day before.

Adapted from Marriage Go Round Manual by F. Russell Crites, Jr.

# Resolution, Compromise or Management
## Handout

| Method of Addressing Conflict | Defined |
|---|---|
| **Resolution** | Resolution is the most preferred method of handling conflict. This simply means that the two of you have come to a conclusion as to how that conflict will be dealt with and both of you feel good about it. |
| **Compromise** | Compromise is the second most preferred method of handling conflict. Compromise occurs when two people consider a variety of solutions and gradually work through the solutions until you come up with one that is acceptable to both people. It may not be exactly what either of you want, but it is acceptable. |
| **Manage** | Managing simply means that neither a resolution or compromise was achieved. However, that doesn't mean that you can manage the conflict. What if you have a conflict and the issue is much more important to one person that it is the other. In such cases you can manage it. Let the person who is most invested have his way and let it go. Keep in mind that the same person cannot always 'win'. To manage simply means that you come up with a workable solution that both of you are willing to accept. Consider the percentage method for this style. If it is 75% important to one person and only 25% important to the other, be willing to let that person who has the greater percentage investment do it his way. It's important that the same person does not always have the highest percentage, or this becomes hurtful instead of helpful. Or you can simply agree to disagree! |

# Conflict Resolution Methods

Conflict resolution occurs when two people come to an agreement that both people are happy with. There are five methods for you to consider using for conflict resolution.

- The Learning Conversation Worksheet*
- The Communication Game
- The Five Step Technique
- Conflict Resolution and Decision-Making Worksheet
- Problem Solving: The Two Column Technique Worksheet

* You may want to work through this before your try anything else. It will help you see the other person's perspective more clearly. This in turn can make resolving a situation much easier.

# The Learning Conversation Worksheet

| | |
|---|---|
| **Describe the Situation:** | |
| **Identify What Happened** | |
| Listen to and explore each other's stories | |
| Share how this bothers you! | |
| What is the other person thinking? | |
| Identify how this bothers or impacts the other person. | |
| Identify how both of your interactions produce this result? | |
| **Identify and understand the underlying feels of both parties!** | |
| Identify and address feelings that both you are experiencing and why.<br>• No judging<br>• No blaming | |
| **Identify how he issue is threatening both your personal identity and the other persons!** | |
| Identify and understand the Identity issues.<br>• Mental Self<br>• Social Self<br>• Physical Self<br>• Spiritual/Moral Self<br>• Feelings | |

Adapted from material in Difficult Conversations: How to Discuss What Matters Most.
If you really want to understand this concept in greater detail I highly recommend that you read the book titled, Difficult Conversations: How to Discuss What Matters Most by Stone, Patton and Heen.

# The Communication Game

## Handout and Exercise

Verbal communication is a method by which we try to let another person know what we think or feel. It is a transference of information from one person to another. This exercise and handout will assist you in developing some basic skills in the area of verbal communication. Follow each step closely.

Instructions:

1. Identify a person who you would like to address a mild to moderate problem with. It would be best to start out with smaller problems until you get use to this method.
2. Identify a small issue that the two of you could discuss that needs to be addressed. You both may want to list up to five issues that could be used. This can be used just to clarify a position, point, or to resolve a conflict.
3. For each issue identified make a short precise statement. One sentence is enough. For example, "I don't think that you understand how tired I am when I get home from work."

| 1st Person's Issues to Be Used | 2nd Person's Issues to be Used |
|---|---|
|  |  |
|  |  |
|  |  |
|  |  |

**STEP ONE:   SENDERS STATEMENT OF WANT OR CONCERN**

The sender makes a specific statement concerning a need, problem, etc. This should be a short, precise statement. For example:

"I don't think you understand how tired I am when I get home from work."

## STEP TWO: RECEIVERS REFLECTION OF COMMUNICATION

The receiver then reflects back word for word if possible, what the sender has stated.

## STEP THREE: SENDERS VERIFICATION OF PROPER REFLECTION

The sender then states either that the receiver correctly or incorrectly reflected the communication. If the communication was not reflected correctly the sender resends the message and the receiver reflects until he gets the message correct.

## STEP FOUR: RECEIVERS CLARIFICATION OF MEANING

The receiver then must ask at least three questions concerning the topic starting with the phrase, "Do you mean...?" You must make three statements that get a "yes" answer from the sender before the clarification step can be considered complete. For example:

"Do you mean that I expect too much from you when you get home?"

IMPORTANT: The receiver can learn valuable information from the "No" and "Yes" responses and can help when you make your summary statement.

## STEP FIVE: SENDERS VERIFICATION OF CLARIFICATION

The sender verifies with only a "Yes" or "No" that the clarification statement is correct. Do not correct, explain, etc. simply say, "Yes" or "No". If you aren't sure, or it's not clear, it's a "No".

## STEP SIX: RECEIVERS SUMMARY STATEMENT

After the receiver makes at least three correct (YES) "Do you mean" statements he then summarizes what he has learned.

## STEP SEVEN: SENDERS VERIFICATION OF SUMMARY

The sender verifies whether or not the receiver accurately understood the communication. If the sender feels that the receiver did not completely understand he/she may then communicate that information to the receiver.

## STEP EIGHT: SENDERS SPECIFIC REQUEST

The sender may then ask the receiver to grant one specific request that would improve the situation.

## STEP NINE: RECIEVERS RESPONSE

If the receiver can't do what the sender requests, then he/she should offer an acceptable alternative. If the receiver accepts the suggested resolution the communication is complete. If not completed go to Step Ten.

## STEP TEN: SENDERS ACCEPTANCE OR NON-ACCEPTANCE

The sender accepts the resolution and says, "Thank you."

The sender does not accept the resolution and the couple tables the situation until they can decide how to resolve it (Look at other Resolution, Compromise or Management options).

---

**Communication Game
Quick Version**

When you the other person speaks and you aren't sure what they mean simply say, "Do you mean….." and see if you get an affirmation that you are correct. If not, ask the person to say it again in a different way!

# The Five Step Conflict Resolution Technique Described

**State the Problem:** The first thing that you must do is accurately define what the problem is and then put it on paper. When you put something on paper it clarifies what you are working on much better than when you simply verbalize it.

**Specifically Describe the Problem:** Go beyond the definition and write down a comprehensive description of the problem that includes specific details. Don't be afraid to over-do the specifics. They are important in the development of good alternatives.

**Brainstorm for Possible Alternatives:** Generate possible solutions to this problem. It is best that you come up with as many solutions as the two of you can before a decision is made.

- Brainstorming is helpful in this stage. Let your imaginations go.
- No negativism or judgments about ideas that either partner thinks up.
- Quantity is desired. The longer your list of alternatives, the more you will have to work with.

**Combine and Improve:** Once you have several ideas go through each one to see if any of them can be combined in order to develop an improved alternative.

- Delete and combine until you have two or three quality alternatives.

**List Each of the Chosen Alternatives:** Put each of the alternatives remaining on a worksheet and determine what the positive and negative consequences for each alternative would be.

# Five Step Technique Conflict Resolution Technique Worksheet

| | |
|---|---|
| **State the Problem:** | |
| **Comprehensive Description:** | |
| **Brainstorm for Possible Alternatives:**<br><br>Use a separate sheet of paper for this step if necessary. Once you have several possibilities, go to the next step. | |
| **Combine, Improve and Delete:** | 1. |
| | 2. |
| | 3. |
| | 4. |
| | 5. |

A copy of this is in the appendices.

| Alternative: | |
|---|---|
| **Positives** | **Negatives** |
| | |
| | |
| | |
| | |
| | |
| | |
| | |
| | |
| | |

# Conflict Resolution and Decision-Making Worksheet

Instructions:

1. Define the conflict in a way that is acceptable to all parties.
2. Write down the choice or alternative that you believe that is best.
3. List the reasons that you believe supports your choice or alternative.

Conflict Defined:_____

Alternative:

Reasons for Choice:

1._____
2._____
3._____
4._____
5._____
6._____
7._____
8._____
9._____
10._____

A copy of this is in the appendices.

# Problem Solving and the Two Column Technique

The next technique is simple yet affective in trying to determine if an alternative is really a good possibility. First you specifically define the problem. Second, you write down the alternative that you want to evaluate. Third, get a piece of paper, put a line down the middle, write positive at the top on one side and negatives on the other side. Once you have done that, simply write down all of the positive and negatives that you can think of. Have someone help you and you'll get a better evaluation of the alternative.

# Problem Solving: The Two Column Technique Worksheet

| **Problem Defined:** ||
|---|---|
| **Selected Possible Alternative:** ||
| **Positives** | **Negatives** |
|  |  |
|  |  |
|  |  |
|  |  |
|  |  |
|  |  |
|  |  |
|  |  |
|  |  |
|  |  |
|  |  |
|  |  |
|  |  |
|  |  |

A copy of this is in the appendices.

# Compromise Methods

Sometimes you need to make sacrifices for people you care for. Sometimes you give in for the betterment of the relationship. Other times, you may not be as invested, and it will be harder to come to a compromise. It may be hard to give in at all. It's important that you think things through so that you can provide options for compromise to anyone you are dealing with. The following are compromise methods that you can consider.

- The Will to Compromise Worksheet
- Compromise Model for Conflict Management Worksheet

# The Will to Compromise

In conflict, there are usually two choices, yours and the other persons. That's why it is often called a conflict. However, could there be a third alternative? If you want to reduce your conflict and improve your relationship with the person, you may want to develop 'The Will to Compromise'. Yes, it is what it means. You should look at both sides of the conflict. Talk to the person and see what his stance is, what his reasons are for his solution, why he feels so strongly about it, etc. You know what you want. You know what your stance is, and it is probably different from the other persons. Now, don't think about what is fair or where the middle might be for the compromise. Think about something you could give in to that would be important to the other person, something that would get his attention and make him see you really want to manage this problem.

1. Identify the other person's solution and write down what (s)he wants to have happen and the reasons why this solution is important to him. Don't make a big deal of it and stay rational. Just gather information. Write what you learn in the left-hand column.
2. Write down your current solution underneath it and the reasons why this solution is important to you. Write your information in the right-hand column.
3. Think about what this other person has shared and why it is important to him. With this in mind, list some possible compromise solutions in the middle column.
4. Once finished, determine if there is a compromise that would meet or partially meet one or more of the other person's reasons for why he prefers his solution.

# The Will to Compromise Worksheet

| Your Partner | The Will to Compromise | You |
|---|---|---|
| Solution:<br><br><br><br><br>**Reasons this is important.** | List your possible compromises. | Your Solution<br><br><br><br><br>**Reasons for the Solution** |
| **I understand that you (reason why his solution is important). Because of that I am willing to:** |||

A copy is in the appendices.

Adapted from Marriage Go Round by F. Russell Crites, Jr.

# Compromise Model for Conflict Management

This model is to be used when you have tried the above mentioned conflict resolution exercises and have determined that you cannot come to a conclusion that both parties can agree on. When this occurs, the next best possibility is to compromise. If you choose this method, there are four basic ground rules if you are going to be effective. First, you must keep in mind that our primary purpose for using this model is to come to an agreement. If you are not willing to come to an agreement, then it is useless to begin this exercise. Second, you both should agree to work through the identified conflict until both agree that they are finished. Third, you need to stay calm and be objective. Last, you need to set a minimum time for the decision to be upheld by both parties.

**Instructions:**

1. Keep in mind that your primary purpose for using this model is to come to an agreement.
2. Both should agree to work through a specific conflict until both agree that they are finished.
3. Stay calm and be objective.
4. Set a minimum time for the decision to be upheld by both parties.

**Step One: Define the Problem!**

Write down the problem in as few words as possible that are acceptable to both parties involved.

**Step Two: Describe Your First Choice!**

Each of you should describe your first choice! Partner #1 briefly states what their first choice is in the resolution of this specific problem. Partner #2 restates the resolution and either agrees or disagrees. If #2 disagrees then he (she) briefly states what their first choice is in the resolution of that specific problem.

**Step Three: Take Turns!**

Each of you take turns proposing alternatives until one of you accepts the others recommendation. Obviously, you must come off of your original suggestion a little at a time until you can come to a conclusion that both of you can live with. The solution may not be what either of you want, but it may be better than completely giving in to the other.

**Step Four: Summarize your agreement!**

Once you have come to an agreement, write down exactly what solution you have come up with in your compromise. This is important since neither of you are extremely happy with the solution. It is easy for people to 'forget' what the solution was or to feel that it was much closer to what they wanted when it hasn't been written down to confirm at a later date.

# Compromise Model for Conflict Worksheet

Instructions:

1. Begin with an agreement that you will focus on protecting each other's feelings and that this is an exercise in helping you both make your life together better, even if it is in a small way.
2. Agree with each other that you will avoid using negative comments, expressing negative feelings and focus on being open, friendly and cooperative in words and deeds.
3. Keep in mind that your primary purpose for using this model is to come to an agreement.
4. Both should agree to work through a specific conflict until both agree that they are finished.
5. Stay calm, take care of each other and take a break if things start to get negative (20-30 Minutes).
   During this time relax and deescalate.
6. Set a minimum time for the decision to be upheld by both parties.

Conflict Defined:_____

Step One: Partner #1 briefly states what their first choice is in the resolution of this specific problem.

Resolution:_____

Partner #2 restates the resolution and either agrees or disagrees. If #2 disagrees then he (she) briefly states what their first choice is in the resolution of that specific problem.

Resolution:_____

Step Two: You continue to propose alternatives until one of you accepts the other's recommendation.

#1_____

#2_____

#1_____

#2_____

#1_____

#2_____

Step Three: Summarize your agreement below.

A copy is in the appendices.

Adapted from Marriage Go Round by F. Russell Crites, Jr.

# Conflict Management Methods

Conflict management is used when neither resolution or compromise is an option. The purpose of conflict management is to come up with a solution that is livable for all parties. It's not easy. However, with some work you can come up with some solutions.

- ➢ Conflict Management Methods
    - Taking Turns
    - It's More about My Life
    - Me First then You
    - Agree to Disagree
    - Let It Go

# Conflict Management Method Options

When all else fails you must find some way to manage the conflict. Obviously, it's much easier to manage conflict that is small and not as important to either one or both parties. However, there will be times when both people (or more) are invested in a solution and no one agrees with the other. Here are some possible alternatives when you are trying to accomplish a workable Conflict Management solution.

1. **Taking Turns:** Let's do it my way this time and we'll do it your way next time.
2. **It's More about My Life:** If you are in charge, we'll do it your way. If I'm in charge, we'll do it my way.
3. **Me First then You:** Let's try my way this time and if it doesn't work, we'll do it your way next time.
4. **Agree to Disagree:** Just don't do this a lot, especially if the issue is important to both of you!
5. **Let It Go:** Simply accept the fact that there will be minor skirmishes and choose to not win one.

**WARNING:** No matter which one you pick, or if you come up with another alternative, it is important that you make the decision and then put it away. Don't hold a grudge. Don't use it against the other person in the future. Just let it go. If you don't you will end up with piles of unresolved conflict that you trip over on a consistent basis and it will cause significant damage in your relationship with the other person. The other option is to simply not have the relationship. In some cases that is very hard to do.

# Keeping Track of Decisions

One of the problems you will face is having to remake decisions that have already been made. After a period of time, you will both have a tendency to remember the decision in a way that is a little different from the other person's perception. To avoid this problem, either use this sheet to record decisions that are made or get a notebook that you would use specifically for writing down decisions that have been made. Call it your Resolution Book for fun.

| Area of Concern | Decision Made | Date |
|---|---|---|
|  |  |  |
|  |  |  |
|  |  |  |
|  |  |  |
|  |  |  |
|  |  |  |

A copy of this is in the appendices.

| Area of Concern | Decision Made | Date |
|---|---|---|
|  |  |  |
|  |  |  |
|  |  |  |
|  |  |  |
|  |  |  |
|  |  |  |
|  |  |  |
|  |  |  |
|  |  |  |

# Conflicts with Personal Decision Making

Conflict doesn't just occur with others. Sometimes we have conflict within ourselves as we attempt to make decisions. When this happens, we need to have a tool that will help us make better decisions. There are several possible decision-making tools that you can use. However, the two methods below will help you with most of the issues you may experience.

- Seven Step Problem Solving Method
- T-Chart for Decision Making

# Seven Step Problem Solving Method

Regardless of what model you used to resolve a problem you are faced with, it is important that you make sure that the solution you have chosen is effective. The following six steps takes you through the process of identifying and determining if the solution you have chosen is effective.

**Step One:** Define the Problem

**Step Two:** Identify Alternative Solutions. Attempt to identity at least three alternative solutions.

**Step Three:** Do a T-chart for each Alternative. See the T-Chart on the next page as a resource. If you feel strongly about one solution, you can always check that one first using the T-Chart.

**Step Four:** Select the solution that appears to be the best option. Usually the best option has more positives and less negatives.

**Step Five:** Implement the solution. As you implement the solution, be open to whether or not it is actually solving your issue.

**Step Six:** Evaluate the solution. If it is working great. You can go forward. If it is not helping as you had hoped, you may need to consider another alternative solution.

**If the solution did not work:**

**Step Seven:** Pick another solution and work through step four through six again. Do this until you identify a solution what is helpful.

# Decision Making T-Chart Worksheet

| Problem or Situation Defined: ||
|---|---|
| Solution Considered: ||
| **Positives Regarding this Solution** | **Negatives Regarding this Solution** |
| | |
| | |
| | |
| | |
| | |
| | |
| | |
| | |
| | |
| | |
| | |

A copy is in the appendices.

# Appendices

- Coping Styles Assessment Quick Check
- Coping Styles Assessment Quick Check Summary
- Developing a DESC Script
- Assertive Techniques Situation Worksheet
- Assertive Script Writing Worksheet
- The Three Step Technique Worksheet
- My Boundaries Worksheet
- Other-Oriented Overt Control and Boundary Damage Worksheet
- Other-Oriented Covert Control and Boundary Damage Worksheet
- Self-Oriented Overt Control and Boundary Damage Worksheet
- Self-Oriented Covert Control and Boundary Damage Worksheet
- Fixing Boundary Issues Worksheet
- Addressing Non-Productive Conflict Styles Worksheet
- Self-Monitoring by Frequency for One Behavior Per Week Form
- The Learning Conversation Worksheet
- Five Step Technique Conflict Resolution Technique Worksheet
- Conflict Resolution and Decision-Making Worksheet
- Problem Solving: The Two Column Technique Worksheet
- The Will to Compromise Worksheet
- Compromise Model for Conflict Worksheet
- Decision Making T-Chart Worksheet

# Coping Styles Assessment
## Quick Check

Name:_____ Age:_____ Sex:_____ Date:_____

**FAMILY OF ORIGIN ROLES**

The below mentioned roles are the most often seen roles in dysfunctional families. Look at each role and determine which one you were most like as a child (when you lived with your parent(s) elementary through High School). If you were not any of these simply do not check anything.

Instructions:

1. Put a check in the left-hand column if you believe you experienced this Family of Origin Role as a child. You can check more than one.
2. Pick the Family of Origin Role that was **most true** for you and put the word '**PRIMARY**' in the column to the right. **You can only choose ONE primary role from the Family of Origin Roles identified**.
3. Pick the Family of Origin Role that was **second most true** for you and put the word, '**SECONDARY**' In the column to the right. **You can only have one secondary Family of Origin Role identified.**

| Check | Family of Origin Roles | Primary and Secondary Role |
|---|---|---|
|  | **THE ENABLER:** The Enabler tries to keep everyone 'fixed'. He constantly helps others to continue in their irresponsibility by rescuing or saving them in some way. |  |
|  | **LITTLE PRINCE(SS):** The Little Prince(ss) often takes on the role of the opposite sex spouse. This child ends up fulfilling the needs of the opposite sex spouse and does not really have a chance at living out their childhood. |  |
|  | **THE ADJUSTER:** The Adjuster agrees with everyone and adapts to every situation. They are extremely flexible and spontaneous. |  |
|  | **THE SCAPEGOAT:** The Scapegoat diverts attention from the family by getting into trouble. |  |
|  | **THE LOST CHILD:** The Lost Child hides out, tries not to make waves, draws attention by non-presence. |  |
|  | **THE MASCOT:** The Mascot lessens tension in the family by being funny or cute. |  |
|  | **THE HERO:** The Hero tries to make the family look good by achieving success in school or work. |  |
|  | **THE PLACATER:** The Placater tries to reduce conflict in the family by smoothing things over. |  |
|  | **THE BOSS:** The Boss attempts to maintain control so that he can do what he believes needs to be done. He wants to be in charge and will make others miserable when he is not. |  |

My Primary Family of Origin Role is:_____ My Secondary Family of Origin Role is:_____

___I have no Family of Origin Roles checked!

## UNHEALTHY COMMUNICATION STYLES

Instructions:

1. Do you exhibit any of the below unhealthy communication styles? If so, put a check in the column on the left.
2. For each unhealthy communication style that you checked on the left look to the right and **select the motivation that appears to be most true for you**. Some motivations are already selected (usually only one motivation for that communication), others have two possibilities. You can only check one motivation per communication style so choose the one that is mostly true for you.

| Check | CODEPENDENT COMMUNICATION STYLE | Primary Motivation |
|---|---|---|
|  | **THE PLACATER:** The Placater is a "yes man". He rarely if ever says, "no" to anyone. When he does, he feels guilty. | Guilt/Shame: Other-Oriented |
|  | **THE BLAMER:** The Blamer rarely takes responsibility for his actions. He constantly blames others for anything negative that happens. | ___Control: Self-Oriented<br>___Avoidant |
|  | **THE COMPUTER:** The Computer is a person of extreme logic. Emotions are expressions of weakness, so they are not to be allowed. | ___Control: Self-Oriented<br>___Avoidant |
|  | **THE DISTRACTER:** The Distracter is the master politician. You can never get a straight answer out of him. He only reveals what he wants to reveal, when he wants to reveal it. | Avoidant |

**Control: Want to do things your way.**
**Avoidant: Find a way to leave, change topics or avoid a conflict.**

## CODEPENDENCY ROLES

Instructions:

1. Do you exhibit this codependency role? If so, put a check in the column on the left.
2. For every codependency that you checked on the left look to the right and select the motivation that appears to be **most true for you**. Some motivations are already selected (usually only one motivation for that codependency), others have two to three possibilities. You can **only check one motivation per codependency** so choose the one that is mostly true for you.

| Check | CODEPENDENCY ROLE | Primary Motivation |
|---|---|---|
|  | **TAP DANCER:** The Tap Dancer finds it difficult to commit to a relationship or to anything else for that matter. | Avoidant |
|  | **PERFECTIONIST:** The Perfectionist has a great deal of difficulty completing things, dealing with people, etc. because everything must be done a certain way to be acceptable. | ___Control: Self-Oriented<br>___Guilt/Shame: Other-Oriented |
|  | **MARTYR:** The Martyr believe that life should be a struggle. As a result, Martyrs often find themselves in situations where they are in pain. | ___Avoidant<br>___Guilt/Shame: Other-Oriented |
|  | **WORKAHOLIC:** The Workaholic has an unhealthy attitude towards achievement. They will often overwork so that they can feel better about their accomplishments. | ___Avoidant<br>___Guilt/Shame: Other-Oriented |
|  | **PEOPLE PLEASER:** The People Pleaser bases his self-esteem on how well he pleases or keeps other people happy. | Guilt/Shame: Other-Oriented |

|   |   |   |
|---|---|---|
|   | **CARETAKER:** The Caretaker prevents the dysfunctional person from experiencing the consequences of his behavior. Caretakers often breed dependence in others. | ____Control: Self-Oriented<br>____Guilt/Shame: Other-Oriented |
|   | **STUMP:** The Stump has a tendency to escape or isolate whenever there are any problems to deal with. | Avoidant |
|   | **LOVE CHILD:** The Love Child is addicted to love. They love too much and as a result their self-esteem is based much on whether or not they are loved. | Guilt/Shame: Other-Oriented |
|   | **COMIC:** The Comic often lessens tension at home, work and play by being funny or cute. Often the Comic uses humor to avoid responsibility, pain, conflict or any other negative emotion or event. | Avoidant |
|   | **CONTROLLER:** The Controller is extremely controlling in his personal relationships. Everything must be done his way or with his permission. | Control: Self-Oriented |
|   | **GOD PLAYER:** The God Player is extremely sensitive to others and often believes that they are responsible for much of what goes on around him. | Guilt/Shame: Other-Oriented |
|   | **REBEL:** This Rebel is often a person who is openly (sometimes passively) defiant or rebellious as an adult. | ____Avoidant<br>____Guilt/Shame: Other-Oriented |

**Guilt/Shame (Other-oriented):** Want to please or get approval from others. **Control (Self-Oriented):** Want to do things your way.
**Avoidant:** Find a way to leave, change topics or avoid a conflict.

**Determination of Motivational Type Predominance**

Look back at your codependencies and at your communication styles. Based on what you see and what you believe about yourself which codependency/communication motivation is the most predominant for you? Keep in mind that you can only check one of the two statements below. If you have multiple checks for one type of codependency that could mean it is more predominant within you.

Is it:

____Self-Oriented Codependency (You **must** have at least **one** **Self-Oriented Codependency/Communication Style** Identified above to check this).

**OR**

____Other-Oriented Codependency (You **must** have at least **one** **Other-Oriented Codependency/Communication** Style Identified above to check this).

**Do NOT** consider the **avoidant codependencies/communications** for the above question!

## UNHEALTHY FAMILY RULES

**Instructions:**

1. Put a check mark next to any Family of Origin Rule that is **currently** causing problems for you.
2. Place a checkmark in the box to the right if it was a problem in your family of Origin. The family you lived with as a child.

| Check | FAMILY OF ORIGIN RULE | Was in Family of Origin |
|---|---|---|
|  | **THE RULE OF RIGIDITY:** The Rule of Rigidity states that as the dysfunction becomes more predominant in the family, the family must become more rigid to compensate for the unpredictability. |  |
|  | **THE RULE OF SILENCE:** The Rule of Silence calls for the family members to remain quiet about the dysfunction in the family. |  |
|  | **THE RULE OF DENIAL:** The rule of denial calls for the family to deny the fact that unhealthy activities are occurring in the family. |  |
|  | **THE RULE OF ISOLATION:** The rule of isolation calls for the family to avoid relationships with others. As the dysfunction becomes more predominant in the family, the family tends to isolate to keep others from finding out what is going on. |  |
|  | **THE RULE OF NON-EMOTION:** The rule of non-emotion calls for family members to avoid talking about feelings. As problems occur it is important that no express how they feel about the issues. Any expression can trigger conflict. |  |
|  | **THE RULE OF TRIANGULATION:** The rule of triangulation calls for family members to communicate to each other through a third party. As the family becomes more dysfunctional it becomes more painful to communicate directly. |  |
|  | **THE RULE OF UNATTAINABLE EXPECTATIONS:** The rule of unattainable expectations puts expectations on family members that promote failure. As the inappropriate behaviors become more prevalent the need for someone in the family to make up for the inadequacies becomes pronounced. |  |
|  | **THE RULE OF OTHER FOCUS:** The rule of other focus calls for family members to focus on the needs of others in hopes of having personal needs met. As the dysfunction progresses it becomes more and more difficult for individuals to communicate that personal needs are not being met. |  |
|  | **THE RULE OF BLIND TRUST:** The rule of blind trust calls for family members to trust each other when reason to trust is in question. Parents communicate that they want their children to do one thing and act the opposite themselves. |  |
|  | **THE RULE OF SEXUAL SILENCE:** The rule of sexual silence calls for family members to maintain silence about any sexual issues. Due to cultural and social avoidance coupled with dysfunctional family rules sex is rarely if ever talked about. |  |
|  | **THE RULE OF SERIOUSNESS:** The rule of seriousness calls for family members to avoid fun and focus on life from a totally rational, objective view point. Parents communicate that they want their children to do one thing and act the opposite themselves. |  |
|  | **THE RULE OF PROJECTED BLAME:** The Rule of Projected blame states that as the disease of alcohol or individual dysfunction becomes more predominant in the individual, he must project the blame or become martyr. Due to the norm of under or over responsibility the individual has a tendency to carry shame that is unnecessary. |  |

**You are finished.** Transfer your scores to the **Coping Styles Assessment Quick Check Summary Page** in order to see your scores on one page.

**IMPORTANT:** If you plan on purchasing the Coping Styles Assessment 80 plus page Codebook through Amazon you will need this assessment data to determine exactly what you need to address in your CODEBOOK. It is also essential that you have your **four-digit code** so that you can purchase the CODEBOOK that is specific to your issues. There are sixteen basic CODEBOOKS and each one has some differences depending on the code that is represented. So, it's important that you order the CODEBOOK that has your specific four-letter code.

This is a list of the sixteen most common codes:

HBOA, HBON, HBSA, HBSN, HUOA, HUON, HUSA, HUSN,
RBOA, RBON, RBSA, RBSN, RUOA, RUON, RUSA, RUSN.

# Coping Styles Assessment
# Quick Check Summary

**My Primary Family of Origin Role was:**_____

**My Secondary Family of Origin Role was:**_____

**Check here if no Role was Identified:**____

**Instructions:**
1. Look back at the Codependency Roles and look to see what motivation you checked for each role. Put that in the graph below so that you can see how many of each types of codependency you have.
2. Look back at the Unhealthy Communication Styles and transfer each motivation you checked in the graph below also.

| Check if it is a Problem | Codependency | Other-Oriented Shame/Guilt Based | Self-Oriented Control Based | Avoidant Based |
|---|---|---|---|---|
| | Tap Dancer | | | X |
| | Perfectionist | | | |
| | Martyr | | | |
| | Workaholic | | | |
| | People Pleaser | X | | |
| | Caretaker | | | |
| | Stump | | | |
| | Love Child | X | | |
| | Comic | | | |
| | Controller | | X | |
| | God Player | | | |
| | Rebel | | | |
| | **Unhealthy Communication Style** | | | |
| | Distractor | | | X |
| | Computer | | | |
| | Blamer | | | |
| | Placater | X | | |

Instructions:
Look back at the Unhealthy Family Rules chart. If the rule is a problem currently check YES below. If not, check NO!

| Unhealthy Family Rule | Currently a Problem | Unhealthy Family Rule | Currently a Problem |
|---|---|---|---|
| Rigidity | ___Yes ___No | Unattainable Expectations | ___Yes ___No |
| Silence | ___Yes ___No | Other Focus | ___Yes ___No |
| Denial | ___Yes ___No | Blind Trust | ___Yes ___No |
| Isolation | ___Yes ___No | Sexual Silence | ___Yes ___No |
| Non-Emotion | ___Yes ___No | Seriousness | ___Yes ___No |
| Triangulation | ___Yes ___No | Projected Blame | ___Yes ___No |

(C) Copyright revision 2019    F. Russell Crites  Report any copyright violations to 972-506-7111

## IDENTIFYING YOUR CODE

**First Code Letter 1:** If you identified a family of origin role that you experienced as a child put a **H** above the number 1 below. If you had no family of origin roles put an **R** above the number 1.

**Second Code Letter 2:**
If you **ONLY** had **Other-Oriented** Codependencies/Unhealthy Communication styles put an **O** above number 2.
If you **ONLY** had **Self-Oriented** Codependencies/Unhealthy Communication styles put an **S** above the number 2.
If you had **BOTH** Other-Oriented and Self-Oriented Codependences/Unhealthy Communication styles put a **B** above number 2.

**Third Code Letter 3:** Look back at **Determination of Motivational Type Predominance** below the Codependency Roles. Did you check **other** or **self** as being more predominant. If it was **Self put an S in the number 3 spot** below. If it **was Other, put an O in the number 3 spot.**

**Fourth Code Letter 4:** If it was checked that you have even one **Avoidant Codependencies or Avoidant Unhealthy Communication styles put an A in the last spot (4)**.
If you have **no Avoidant Codependencies or Avoidant Communication styles put an N on the last spot (4)**.

Your Person Treatment Code is:   ____ ____ ____ ____
                                   1    2    3    4

Your Boundary Code is the last three letters in your Code:   ____ ____ ____
                                                              2    3    4

# Developing a DESC Script

There are four basic steps in developing a D(escibe) E(xpress) S(pecify) C(onsequence) script. Whenever you are faced with a situation where you feel you might be controlled or manipulated by another person, use script writing to help you.

Your Scenario:

Describe:

Express:

Specify:

Consequence (Choose positive or negative or both):

Permission to copy for personal use by the individual purchasing this workbook.

# Assertive Techniques Situation Worksheet

Instructions

1. When you are faced with a situation you need to address using an assertive technique, you can use this worksheet.
2. Identify the situation.
3. Pick the Assertive Technique that you want to use.
4. Write a statement that addresses the issue using the chosen assertive technique.

| Assertive Techniques Situation Worksheet |
|---|
| **Situation Described:** |
| **Specific Assertive Technique to Be Used:** |
| **Assertive Statement:** |

Permission to copy for personal use by the individual purchasing this workbook.

# Assertive Script Writing Worksheet

Instructions

1. Describe the situation in the space provided below.
2. Name the person you want to alter the situation with.
3. Describe the setting--the place it usually takes place.
4. Write down what the you usually say to them.
5. Write down a counter script that states exactly what you want to Communicate. You can include the persons normal response that is unacceptable if desired.

| **Assertive Script Writing Worksheet** ||
| --- | --- |
| Step #1. | Describe the Situation! |
| Step #2. | Name the Person you want to alter the situation with. |
| Step #3. | Describe the setting--the place it usually takes place. |
| Step #4. | Write down what the you usually say to them. |
| Step #5. | Write down a counter script that states exactly what you want to Communicate. You can include the persons normal response that is unacceptable if desired. |

Permission to copy for personal use by the individual purchasing this workbook.

# The Three Step Technique Worksheet

The three-step technique is designed for situations where you lack the time or energy to prepare a longer script or where a simple assertive technique won't do enough. This assertive technique can be shortened to three basic statements. Using a personal situation write out a three-step assertive technique for something that is causing you distress or problems. Do two if you like.

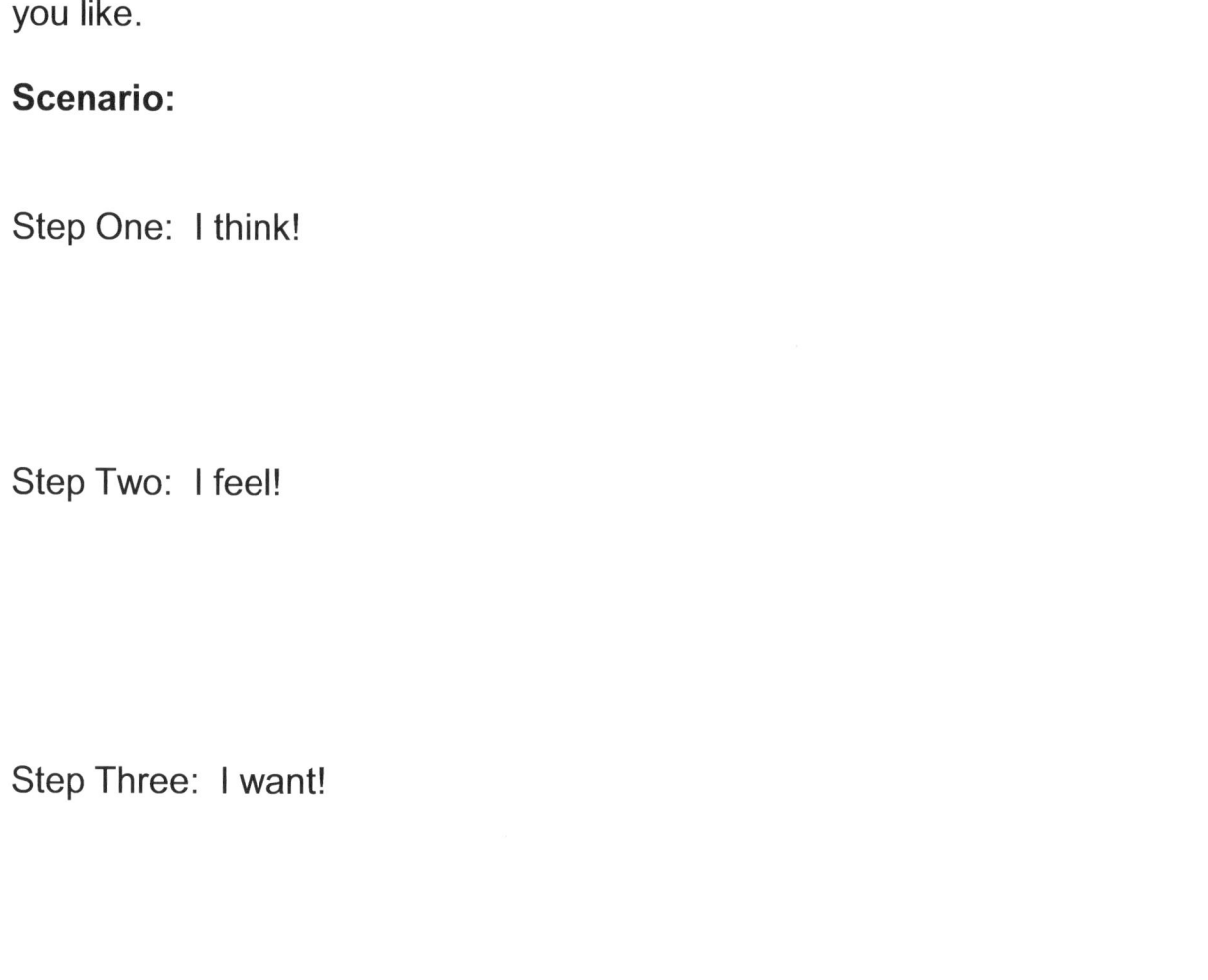

**Scenario:**

Step One: I think!

Step Two: I feel!

Step Three: I want!

Permission to copy for personal use by the individual purchasing this workbook.

# My Boundaries Worksheet

**Instructions**

1. Place the issue or boundary need in the left-hand column.
2. Identify the boundary you want to set in the right-hand column.
3. Make sure to include a consequence if someone tests your boundary.

## Personal Boundaries

| Boundary Need | Boundary |
|---|---|
|  |  |
|  |  |
|  |  |
|  |  |
|  |  |
|  |  |
|  |  |
|  |  |
|  |  |

Permission to copy for personal use by the individual purchasing this workbook.

# Other-Oriented Overt Control and Boundary Damage Worksheet

**Instructions**

1. Write down the covert control that either you use against others or that others use against you.
2. Write down how you will attempt to address this form of covert control next time

| **Addressing Overt Control** ||
|---|---|
| Overt Control Type: | |
| Write down an example of a situation where this has been used against you: | |
| Write down what your response is in that situation and what usually happens. | |
| Identify an assertive technique that you could use to counter that covert control type if it occurs again in the future. | |
| Write down exactly how you would use that technique if this situation occurs again. | |

Permission to copy for personal use by the individual purchasing this workbook.

# Other-Oriented Covert Control and Boundary Damage Worksheet

**Instructions**

1. Write down the covert control that either you use against others or that others use against you.
2. Write down how you will attempt to address this form of covert control next time

| Addressing Covert Control | |
|---|---|
| Covert Control Type: | |
| Write down an example of a situation where this has been used against you: | |
| Write down what your response in that situation and what usually happens. | |
| Identify an assertive technique that you could use to counter that covert control type if it occurs again in the future. | |
| Write down exactly how you would use that technique if this situation occurs again. | |

Permission to copy for personal use by the individual purchasing this workbook.

# Self-Oriented Overt Control and Boundary Damage Worksheet

**Instructions**

1. Write down the overt control that either you use against others.
2. Write down how you will attempt to reduce this form of overt control next time

| | Reducing Overt Control |
|---|---|
| Overt Control Type: | |
| Write down an example of a Situation where you have used this with another person. | |
| Write down what the other person usually says or does in that situation and what usually happens. | |
| What can you do to reduce this particular type of overt control in similar situations in the future? | |
| Write down exactly how you would respond in a reasonable way that does not include any form of control. What words would you use to respond? | |

Permission to copy for personal use by the individual purchasing this workbook.

# Self-Oriented Covert Control and Boundary Damage Worksheet

**Instructions**

1. Write down the covert control that either you use against others.
2. Write down how you will attempt to reduce this form of covert control next time

| Reducing Covert Control | |
|---|---|
| Covert Control Type: | |
| Write down an example of a Situation where you have used this with another person. | |
| Write down what the other person usually says or does in that situation and what usually happens. | |
| What can you do to reduce this particular type of covert control in similar situations in the future? | |
| Write down exactly how you would respond in a reasonable way that does not include any form of control. What words would you use to respond? | |

Permission to copy for personal use by the individual purchasing this workbook.

## Fixing Boundary Issues Worksheet

| Boundary Issue Identified | How I will fix it! |
|---|---|
|  |  |
|  |  |
|  |  |
|  |  |
|  |  |
|  |  |
|  |  |

Permission to copy for personal use by the individual purchasing this workbook.

# Addressing Non-Productive Conflict Styles Worksheet

**Relationships:** Which style does a person you often deal with in life exhibit? List the person and the non-productive style that is used!

| Relationship | Person's Name | Non-Productive Style Used |
|---|---|---|
| Family Member | | |
| A Significant Someone | | |
| A Close Friend | | |
| Someone at Work | | |
| Other: | | |

Instructions

1. Identify the person and the non-productive style used
2. Identify the assertive method you may want to use to minimize the other person's usage of that non-productive style with you!
3. Pick a preferred Conflict method you would want to use in such situations. Keep in mind that you won't always be able to use the one you want, you may have to adjust.

| Person | Non-Productive Style Used | Assertive Method to Use to Address it. | Preferred Conflict Method to use instead. |
|---|---|---|---|
| | | | |
| | | | |
| | | | |
| | | | |

**Relationships:** Which style do you often use with others? List the specific person and the non-productive style that you use with that person!

| Relationship | Person's Name | Non-Productive Style Used |
|---|---|---|
| Family Member | | |
| Significant Someone | | |
| A Close Friend | | |
| Someone at Work | | |
| Other: | | |

Permission to copy for personal use by the individual purchasing this workbook.

# Self-Monitoring by Frequency for One Behavior Per Week Form

**Name:**                                  **Beginning Date:**

## Instructions

1. Prepare yourself and start on a Sunday so that you can more easily keep track for specific weeks at a time.
2. Write down the behavior or words you are wanting to reduce the frequency of in the space provided.
3. Mark across the number each time you exhibit the behavior you are trying to reduce.
4. You probably won't exhibit one of the chosen behaviors ten times in a day. It is possible, but not probable. If it did happen simply put a Plus sign + next to the 10 to show that you exhibited that behavior more than ten times.
5. The goal is to reduce the times you exhibit the behavior or use the words that has caused you or other's problems.

| Behavior to be Measured | |
|---|---|
| **Day** | **Times Exhibited Today** |
| Sunday | 1   2   3   4   5   6   7   8   9   10 |
| Monday | 1   2   3   4   5   6   7   8   9   10 |
| Tuesday | 1   2   3   4   5   6   7   8   9   10 |
| Wednesday | 1   2   3   4   5   6   7   8   9   10 |
| Thursday | 1   2   3   4   5   6   7   8   9   10 |
| Friday | 1   2   3   4   5   6   7   8   9   10 |
| Saturday | 1   2   3   4   5   6   7   8   9   10 |

Permission to copy for personal use by the individual purchasing this workbook.

# The Learning Conversation Worksheet

| | |
|---|---|
| **Describe the Situation:** | |
| **Identify What Happened** | |
| Listen to and explore each other's stories | |
| Share how this bothers you! | |
| What is the other person thinking? | |
| Identify how this bothers or impacts the other person. | |
| Identify how both of your interactions produce this result? | |
| **Identify and understand the underlying feels of both parties!** | |
| Identify and address feelings that both you are experiencing and why.<br>• No judging<br>• No blaming | |
| **Identify how he issue is threatening both your personal identity and the other persons!** | |
| Identify and understand the Identity issues.<br>• Mental Self<br>• Social Self<br>• Physical Self<br>• Spiritual/Moral Self<br>• Feelings | |

Adated from material in Difficult Conversations: How to Discuss What Matters Most.
Permission to copy for personal use by the individual purchasing this workbook.

# Five Step Technique Conflict Resolution Technique Worksheet

| | |
|---|---|
| **State the Problem:** | |
| **Comprehensive Description:** | |
| **Brainstorm for Possible Alternatives:**<br><br>Use a separate sheet of paper for this step if necessary. Once you have several possibilities go to the next step. | |
| **Combine, Improve and Delete:** | 1. |
| | 2. |
| | 3. |
| | 4. |
| | 5. |

Permission to copy for personal use by the individual purchasing this workbook.

**Alternative:**

| Positives | Negatives |
|---|---|
|  |  |
|  |  |
|  |  |
|  |  |
|  |  |
|  |  |
|  |  |
|  |  |
|  |  |

Permission to copy for personal use by the individual purchasing this workbook.

# Conflict Resolution and Decision-Making Worksheet

Instructions:

1. Define the conflict in a way that is acceptable to all parties.
2. Write down the choice or alternative that you believe that is best.
3. List the reasons that you believe supports your choice or alternative.

Conflict Defined:_____

Alternative:

Reasons for Choice:

1._____

2._____

3._____

4._____

5._____

6._____

7._____

8._____

9._____

10._____

Permission to copy for personal use by the individual purchasing this workbook.

# Problem Solving: The Two Column Technique Worksheet

**Problem Defined:**

**Selected Possible Alternative:**

| Positives | Negatives |
|---|---|
|   |   |
|   |   |
|   |   |
|   |   |
|   |   |
|   |   |
|   |   |
|   |   |
|   |   |
|   |   |
|   |   |
|   |   |
|   |   |
|   |   |

Permission to copy for personal use by the individual purchasing this workbook.

# The Will to Compromise Worksheet

| Your Partner | The Will to Compromise | You |
|---|---|---|
| **Solution:**<br><br><br><br><br>**Reasons this is important.** | List your possible compromises. | Your Solution<br><br><br><br><br>Reasons for the Solution |
| **I understand that you (reason why his solution is important). Because of that I am willing to:** |||

Permission to copy for personal use by the individual purchasing this workbook.

# Compromise Model for Conflict Worksheet

Instructions:

1. Begin with an agreement that you will focus on protecting each other's feelings and that this is an exercise in helping you both make your life together better, even if it is in a small way.
2. Agree with each other that you will avoid using negative comments, expressing negative feelings and focus on being open, friendly and cooperative in words and deeds.
3. Keep in mind that your primary purpose for using this model is to come to an agreement.
4. Both should agree to work through a specific conflict until both agree that they are finished.
5. Stay calm, take care of each other and take a break if things start to get negative (20-30 Minutes).
During this time relax and deescalate.
6. Set a minimum time for the decision to be upheld by both parties.

Conflict Defined:_____


Step One: Partner #1 briefly states what their first choice is in the resolution of this specific problem.

Resolution:_____

    Partner #2 restates the resolution and either agrees or disagrees. If #2 disagrees then he (she) briefly states what their first choice is in the resolution of that specific problem.

Resolution:_____

Step Two: You continue to propose alternatives until one of you accepts the other's recommendation.

#1_____

#2_____

#1_____

#2_____

#1_____

#2_____

Step Three: Summarize your agreement below.

# Decision Making T-Chart Worksheet

| Problem or Situation Defined: ||
|---|---|
| Solution Considered: ||
| **Positives Regarding this Solution** | **Negatives Regarding this Solution** |
|  |  |
|  |  |
|  |  |
|  |  |
|  |  |
|  |  |
|  |  |
|  |  |
|  |  |
|  |  |
|  |  |

Permission to copy for personal use by the individual purchasing this workbook.

# Recommended Readings

Allen, James  As a Man Thinketh.  Originally Published in 1903.  Can be downloaded from internet or purchased in book form.

Bower, A., Bower, G.  Asserting Yourself:  A Practical Guide for Positive Change. Reading, MA: Addison-Wesley Publishing Company, 1992.

Coué, Emile  Self-Mastery Through Conscious Autosuggestion.  Originally published in 1922.  Can be down loaded from internet or purchased in book form.

Crites, Jr. F. Russell  Adult Child Therapy Manual:  Counseling Individuals Who Come From Dysfunctional Families - Revised.  Dallas, TX: CPC, 2016.

Crites, Jr. F. Russell  Family Therapy Manual: A Pragmatic Approach to Addressing Dysfunctional Family Issues – Revised.  Dallas, TX:  CPC, 2016.

Crites, Jr. F. Russell  Assertiveness, Boundaries and Conflict Resolution workbook:  ABC Workbook.  Manuscript.

Crites, Jr. F. Russell  HBOA Codebook - Revised.  Dallas, TX:  CPC, 2016.

Dusek JA, Benson H. Mind-body medicine: a model of the comparative clinical impact of the acute stress and relaxation responses. Minnesota Medicine. 2009;92(5):47–50.

Gabor, D.  How to Start a Conversation and Make Friends.  New York, NY: Simon & Schuster, 2011.

Hoffart, Marita B. PhD, RN; Keene, Elizabeth Pross MS, RN   The Benefits of VISUALIZATION: Research suggests that visualization promotes relaxation, enhances sleep, reduces pain, and increases creativity.  AJN, American Journal of Nursing: December 1998 - Volume 98 - Issue 12 - ppg 44-47

Maltz, Maxwell    Psycho-Cybernetics: A New Technique for Using Your Subconscious Power. Englewood Cliffs, NJ: Prentice-Hall, 1960.

Marshall, Grant N.; Wortman, Camille B.; Kusulas, Jeffrey W.; Hervig, Linda K.; Vickers Jr., Ross R. Distinguishing optimism from pessimism: Relations to fundamental dimensions of mood and personality. Journal of Personality and Social Psychology, Vol 62(6), Jun 1992, 1067-1074

Rasmussen, Heather N., Scheier, Michael F., Greenhouse, Joel B. Optimism and Physical Health: A Meta-analytic Review Annals of Behavioral Medicine June 2009, 37:239

Seligman, M. Learned Optimism: How to Change Your Mind and Your Life. New York, NY: Vintage Books, 2006.

Smith, M. J. When I Say No, I Feel Guilty: How to Cope, Using the Skills of Systematic Assertive Therapy. New York, NY: Bantam Books, 1975.

Stone, D., Patton, B., & Heen, S. Difficult Conversations: How to Discuss What Matters Most NY, NY: Penguin Books, 2000.

# Other Works by this Author

**Adult Child Therapy Manual: Counseling Individuals who come from Dysfunctional Families - Revised.** This 200 plus page manual includes forms and therapy aids, diagnostic tools, how to identify and resolve family of origin issues, addresses adult child issues, show you how to identify and resolve codependency issues, how to deal with past issues, how to change thinking and habits, and how visualizations, affirmations other methods that will help your client experience positive change and more. This manual is available on Amazon, through your local bookstore or can be purchased from the author.

**Adult Child Therapy Workbook:** This workbook included the Adult Child Assessment which measures over thirty adult child characteristics that can cause individuals difficulties. There are worksheets for each of the characteristics identified in the assessment as well as several helpful strategies. This workbook is available on Amazon, through your local bookstore or can be purchased from the author.

**Assertiveness, Boundaries and Conflict Management – Revised Workbook:** This workbook covers assertiveness skills, how to set healthy boundaries in a multitude of situations, and how to address conflict. Three methods are addressed; Conflict Resolution, Conflict Compromise and Conflict Management. This workbook is available on Amazon, through your local bookstore or can be purchased from the author.

**Attention Deficit/Hyperactivity Disorder: The Ultimate Guide for Parents of ADHD Children & Adolescents.** This book provides parents with the tools needed to help their child with hyperactivity, impulsivity and inattentive issues. It also addresses executive function or brain-based issues that often cause significant issues for any child experiencing ADHD. Some of the executive functions addressed are planning, time management, prioritization, getting on task, staying on task, organization and emotional control. This book will be available soon on Amazon or at your local bookstore!

**Bipolar Disorder Survival Workbook: Maximize Health While Minimizing Depression and Mania.** This workbook is intended to be a daily aid in helping any person who has Bipolar disorder. A daily chart helps the individual determine if he is doing well, beginning to get depressed, anxious, hypomanic/manic, or beginning to experience hallucinations. Strategies are offered to address each of these areas in order to minimize the negative effect. In addition, the chart also helps the person see if he is sleeping when he should, whether or not he is eating properly, if stress is present and more in order to give him the best chance to have a good day. This can also be a helpful tool for parents and counselors who work with children and adolescents who are experiencing bipolar issues. This workbook is available on Amazon, through your local bookstore or can be purchased from the author.

**Bipolar or ADHD: Educational and Home-Based Strategies for Bipolar Disorder, ADHD and other Co-Existing Conditions.** This book covers the different types of bipolar disorder, strategies for elementary and secondary students, how to reduce mood swings and rage states, how to teach students to self-monitor, and a disciplinary model for home and school. It also addresses ADHD, Anxiety, Depression, Oppositional Defiant, Conduct Disorder and more. Strategies to address these issues are also included. This book is available on Amazon, through your local bookstore or can be purchased from the author.

**CODE books for the Coping Styles Assessment**. There are sixteen different CODE books available and are based on the data obtained from the **Coping Styles Assessment,** or the **Coping Styles Quick Check** assessment. The code books address the following issues: 1) Nine Family of Origin Roles, 2) Twelve Family of Origin Rules in both past and present families, 3) Twelve Codependency Roles, 4) Four Unhealthy Communication Styles, 5) Three Underlying Motivations (Self-Oriented Control, Other-Oriented Accommodation, and Avoidance), 6) Neglect and Abuse Issues, 7) Control Issues and more depending on the code. It also addresses the unique concept of Bipolar Codependency for those who scores suggest it is an issue. The following codes are possible: HBOA, HBON, HUOA, HUON, HBSA, HBSN, HUSA, HUSN, RBOA, RBON, RUOA, RUON, RBSA, RBSN, RUSA, RUSN. These workbooks are available on Amazon, through your local bookstore or can be purchased from the author.

**Depression and Anxiety in Students: Strategies for Counselors and Teachers.** This is a power packed strategy guide that both counselors and teachers can use to positively impact students who have depression or anxiety. Different types of anxiety are addressed. This book is available on Amazon, through your local bookstore or can be purchased from the author.

**Depression and Anxiety in Adults: Self-Help Tools for Addressing Depression and Anxiety.** This workbook provides the counselor or concerned individual with a variety of techniques and strategies that can help with both depression and anxiety. The techniques have been taken from a variety of counseling systems as has the strategies and accommodations included in this workbook. Within this work is a multitude of strategies that can be used to help deal with depression and/or anxiety. It's important to note that there are several strategies that can be used for both depression and anxiety. Find what works for you and use it. This book is available on Amazon, through your local bookstore or can be purchased from the author.

**Family Therapy Manual: A Pragmatic Approach to Addressing Dysfunctional Family Issues – Revised.** This 200 plus page manual includes Assessment tools for working with families, forms and therapy aids, information on Dysfunctional Family Roles, Strategies to Promote a Healthy Family, Promoting Healthy Family Traits, Dysfunctional Family Rules, Teaching Values and Parenting, Discipline and more. This manual is available on Amazon, through your local bookstore or can be purchased from the author.

**Foundations Workbook – Revised.** This workbook assists the person as he attempts to identify a healthy sense of self. Mental, Social, Physical and Spiritual/Moral and Emotional aspects of self are addressed. Strategies to improve in all areas are provided. Foundations, which is core in the Genesis System for Self-Improvement, is also discussed in detail. Foundations includes sections on how to take your mind back. You will learn how to control what you think and when you think it instead of having your mind run amuk and produce chaos, anxiety and frustration. Next, Foundations teaches you the strategies necessary for you to reprogram your unconscious mind. Unhealthy imbedded beliefs often control what you think, say and do. You will learn how to change these unhealthy imbedded beliefs so that your mind will direct you toward new healthier thoughts, words and actions. To help with this, a method called the Inner Sanctum is discussed and taught. Using the Inner Sanctum you can begin to produce change at a deeper more powerful way. This manual is available on Amazon, through your local bookstore or can be purchased from the author.

**Homework Assignments and Project Planning Forms Workbook.** This is a planner for students that will help them keep track of homework, projects, keep other classmates phone numbers and generally help them keep track of necessary information to do well in school. It also has a teacher check off for homework to make sure it has been written down. This is highly recommended for any student who has ADHD or any Executive function issue. This workbook is available on Amazon, through your local bookstore or can be purchased from the author.

**Kids Under Construction: Help for the Strong-Willed Child Workbook.** This workbook provides information and tools for parents or counselors who work with a child who is strong-willed or out of control. The system includes how to establish consequences, rewards, as well as parent tools for discipline. In addition, responsibility development is encouraged by teaching children good self-judgment and self-discipline skills. Children also learn the value of money and how important a good work ethic can be in their lives. This workbook is available on Amazon, through your local bookstore or can be purchased from the author.

**Marriage Go Round: The First Journey – A Therapeutic Guide for Helping Couples Heal and Rekindle Love in Their Lives.** This manual includes forms and therapy aids, what to do when only one partner comes to therapy, a discussion of relationship cycles, identifies and discusses the stages of relationship, addresses the necessity for change, conflict resolution or management, forgiveness and reconciliation, how to reactivate an individual's emotional core, three foundational pillars (Commitment, Partner being a Priority, Service). Eight specific issues are addressed in this manual. However, thirty-two specific love expectations are identified using the Marriage Go Round Assessment. These thirty-two different expectations are assessed and prioritized for each person in the relationship. Some of the areas addressed are Trust, Romance, Physical Affection, Admiration, Having Fun, Emotional Connection, Finances, Communication, Appreciation, Honesty, personal Space, Respect, Spiritual Unity, Sexuality and Sexual Affection. Worksheets, strategies, handouts, individual and couple exercises are all part of the system. This manual is available on Amazon, through your local bookstore or can be purchased from the author.

**Couple Therapy Resources: Assessments and Advanced Materials for Helping Couples Heal and Rekindle Love in Their Lives:** This manual has over 300 plus pages of worksheets, strategies, handouts, individual and couple exercises. While the first manual covers some basic foundational material, The Second manual covers all thirty-two identified love expectations. This manual is available on Amazon, through your local bookstore or can be purchased from the author.

**Marriage Go Round Basic Workbook: Nine Steps to Improving Your Relationship and Rekindling Love in Your life.** This is the companion workbook that clients can use in a therapy situation. Therapists may purchase multiple copies at a discount through the author, or can buy them individually through Amazon. This manual is available on Amazon, through your local bookstore or can be purchased from the author.

**Three Faces of Codependency:** This is the book that communicates the underlying principles of codependency. It's unique in that it addresses three types of codependency along with specific underlying motivations. Once identified it also helps the individual understand how codependency negatively impacts day to day life. Sixteen different codependency code workbooks are available that helps the reader work more thoroughly through his identified issues. There is a quick test for codependency issues in the book. However, a much longer and more informative assessment that can be purchased through this author (see Coping Styles Assessment). This book is available on Amazon, through your local bookstore or can be purchased from the author.

**Twelve Step Workbook – Revised:** This particular workbook addresses the twelve steps that may be taken to help you heal more efficiently. The steps are broken down to show whether or not there is an internal, an external element to each step. Some steps actually require both an internal and external response. Regardless, this work is extremely practical and provides helpful worksheets that can be used over and over again as needed. This work also includes a segment entitled Foundations. Foundations is a core element of the Genesis System for Self-Improvement. Foundations teaches you the strategies necessary for you to reprogram your unconscious mind. Unhealthy embedded beliefs often control what you think, say and do. You will learn how to change these unhealthy embedded beliefs so that your mind will direct you toward new healthier thoughts, words and actions. To help with this a method called the Inner Sanctum is discussed and taught. Using the Inner Sanctum you can begin to produce change at a deeper more powerful way. This workbook is available on Amazon, through your local bookstore or can be purchased from the author.

**NOTE:** Workbooks can be purchased at a discount for therapists who wish to resell them for therapy use. Call author for more information.

**SEMINAR OR CONTACT INFORMATION**

Anyone interested in hosting a training seminar for dealing with personal issues and codependency or any other program specific to the materials listed above please contact:

F. Russell Crites, M.S., LPC, LMFT, LSSP, NBCCH, CPC
Crites Counseling and Consultation
106 N. Denton Tap Rd. Ste 210-216
Coppell, Texas  75019

www.critescounseling.com
See Amazon Author Central:  amazon.com/author/russcrites
972-506-7111

Printed in Great Britain
by Amazon